A GUIDE F[...]
—WHO FEE[...]STUCK —

SO NOW
WHAT?

CATHERINE A. BRENNAN

ISBN 13: 978-1-63489-296-4
eISBN: 978-1-63489-303-9

Library of Congress Catalog Number: 2019917409
Printed in the United States of America
First Printing: 2020

24 23 22 21 20   5 4 3 2 1

Cover design by Nupoor Gordon

Wise Ink Creative Publishing
807 Broadway St NE
Suite 46
Minneapolis, MN, 55413

To order, visit www.itascabooks.com or call 1-800-901-3480.
Reseller discounts available.

To my husband, Mike.
Your generous spirit
shows the power of love.
Your persistence in the face
of struggles is beyond compare.
You have never let go of my hand.
I love you.

CONTENTS

INTRODUCTION

You're never stuck, you're just afraid of doing what's next.
—Wyatt Webb

We want to look good, feel good, and do good. We want to be able to move through life with energy and vitality, manage our emotions with understanding and maturity, and have a sense of purpose, hope, and peace.

It's all possible.

But life throws curveballs at us, and we're not sure how to handle them. Suddenly we are battling illnesses, reacting to the bad news around us, and becoming cynical about the future. These curveballs were given to us for growth. Each one will either strengthen or weaken us.

It's our choice.

It becomes too much. We feel like someone has dished up more than we can handle. We develop coping mechanisms to minimize the damage and pain. We back into a corner, lower our head, sink down to the floor, and protect ourselves with our arms.

We're stuck.

STUCK

We all experience it. We find ourselves sad, without energy or hope. We bump up against a wall and don't know what to do next. We feel cornered as our health fails, our relationships crumble, or we can't get our head around what's in front of us. We're stuck.

Stuck is a place where we're confused, overwhelmed, or trapped. Moving seems like attempting to walk the high wire across Niagara Falls; our feet, mind, and heart fail us. There seems to be no solution, so we resign ourselves to the status quo and shrink back from the challenge.

This is stuck.

When we are stuck, we live a humdrum life. We play it safe and aren't able to fully enjoy the benefits of who we were created to be—and neither is anyone else.

Unstuck is a place of physical strength, limberness, and energy. You can function in your life without restrictions, feel well rested, live an active life, and enjoy the food you eat.

Unstuck is being mentally strong, with relationships beyond simple agreement. It's the ability to meet challenges and have a confident sense of self, positive mind, and good work ethic. It means being curious, strong in stressful situations, hopeful in difficulty, and a pleasure to be around.

Unstuck is being spiritually content, peaceful, hopeful, joyful, loving, faithful, and grateful. It's the ability to find meaning in the events of life, not being threatened by others' differing beliefs, and being part of the fabric of humanity by embracing others and self. Unstuck is concerned with others and living with a purpose.

Does this sound too good to be true?

It's not.

From Stuck to Freedom

Let me tell you a little of my story. I was stuck in the ocean of depression for thirty-five years. From adolescence to my late forties, my world was scary and out of control. My body was tired, my mind frazzled, and my soul sad. I was definitely stuck and didn't know how to get out.

And it wasn't as if I weren't trying.

When I was depressed, my body didn't function right; my mind was a swirling mess of twisted, negative thoughts; and I didn't think I was worthy of love from God. I had a pile of excuses for why my life was so bad. Fear drove me to make limited and small decisions. I felt buried under a mountain of things I "should" do and concerns of the world. On the flip side, I didn't believe I was capable of solving my own problems, and I sat waiting for others to rescue me from my misery.

Several medical professionals suggested I "go out and make some friends." "Join a health club," they suggested as a weak attempt to move me in the right direction. They may as well have been asking me to climb Mt. Everest or swim the English Channel. I had no energy or motivation to go clubbing.

After listening to my complaints, a courageous friend asked if I had ever thought of hurting myself. My answer was the first piece to the puzzle of what had me stuck. She told me my self-destructive thoughts were not normal and pleaded with me to see another doctor. Having promised her, I went and received a diagnosis.

Clinical depression.

Over time, I discovered being stuck under the force of this disease meant the battle was mine alone. No one else could do the work. But little did I know, I would learn amazing lessons along this journey. I want to share them with you.

Depression is not simply a mental health disease. My poor physical and spiritual health were equal partners. The first step was to start eating right, which allowed me to feel good enough to begin working on my mental health. The last piece involved redefining my spiritual world as a recipient of love instead of judgment.

You may not suffer from depression, but the principle is the same for you. There's no need to suffer. Whatever has you stuck, can be overcome. You can be free.

FREEDOM

Once depression no longer owned me, I had freedom. Living in a body that was now healthy and a mind unencumbered by sadness allowed me to get even stronger. My spirit was now free to love, my mind free to dream, and my body free to run.

When my neighbor decided to run a marathon, I volunteered to help on race day. Looking into the faces of men and women, young and old, big and small, I was inspired to try running. A year later, I ran a half marathon.

It changed my life.

It can be the same for you. Getting unstuck will set you free. The possibilities are endless.

SHOULD WE STAY OR SHOULD WE GO?

There are just as many reasons to stay stuck as there are to get unstuck. Our minds can be very creative in shielding us from the short-term effort, even if it would lead to a good long-term result. None of us want to work *that* hard unless we're assured of winning the jackpot.

Your first step to getting unstuck is to identify what "staying stuck" is keeping you from, such as, *I'm not able to play because I'm sore/inflexible/overweight, I'm not able to stay in a relationship, I'm not motivated because I'm gloomy about the future,* or *I don't have enough time, energy, or money.*

When we take a good look at what we're missing by staying

stuck, motivation begins to take hold. Simply understanding the steps to gaining freedom will make the process possible. And not only that; other people will benefit from you getting unstuck as well.

OVERVIEW

There are many reasons we get stuck. They include our fears, feelings, and beliefs. They cause us to be weak, overwhelmed, and disappointed. They cause us to have the wrong focus and leave us without solutions for our problems. But the most compelling reason we're stuck? We won't take a step forward.

To gain freedom, we need to make a conscious choice, figure out what being stuck is keeping us from, and learn the necessary skills. Then we can bless others with our gifts and live a fulfilled life.

Once you know how to do this and make a commitment to yourself, the rest is easy. Unstuck is healthy. Unstuck is free. It's encompassing a deep understanding of how each of the three elements—physical, mental, and spiritual—affects the others. No doctor, counselor, or clergyperson has it all figured out. Getting unstuck involves being in balance and pursuing our physical, mental, *and* spiritual health.

PRACTICE

Just as we need to perceive height, width, and depth to see in three dimensions, we need to add physical, mental, and spiritual practices to our life to fully enjoy it. Taking small steps in all three of these areas will give you the best and fastest results. Focusing only on physical health may help you lose five pounds, but you won't sustain the weight loss without the mental skills to get rid of excuses and a spiritual reason to treat yourself better.

Physical Health: The underlying cause of my depression was a poor diet. No kidding. Once I started to eat right, I was able to enjoy running, biking, and swimming. I had more energy, and my digestive system began to work.

Each of us needs to eat right, move enough, and get sufficient sleep. There is no way around it. The good news is you don't need to suffer by eating meals that taste like cardboard, be constantly sore from doing squats, or miss out on the fun. You can form a lifestyle where you feel energetic and positive every day simply because the body you live in is working properly. It allows you to enjoy food, gain energy, and feel rested.

Mental Health: It's probably not difficult to imagine I had poor mental health skills when I was depressed. When I began to learn healthy habits instead of destructive ones, I developed confidence and a clear sense of truth.

Your mental health depends on you. Too often we blame others or circumstances for our sad state when the truth is that we get to choose our attitudes and emotions each day. Developing deep connections with others, being inspired by those you admire, setting personal boundaries, and engaging in positive self-talk are just a few of the ways to boost your mental and emotional muscles.

Spiritual Health: I had been a "religious" person my whole life, but my misunderstandings of what it required left me without the strength and knowledge necessary to show love, have hope, and be grateful.

We are all spiritual beings, and it's critical to understand this. Religious institutions may or may not be the place you feed your spirit, but they can help us grow. When we practice the seven spiritual practices of faith, gratitude, hope, joy, love, meaning, and purpose, we get unstuck from our cynicism and hopelessness.

And finally, your physical, mental, and spiritual health impact one another. You will experience exponential benefits when you get healthy in all three areas. Sometimes, what may seem like the most obvious way to get unstuck is not it at all.

In my case, working on my mental health to alleviate my depression wasn't the right place to start. My physical health had to be addressed first because my sick body was affecting my mind. It may be the same with you too. As you begin to see the connections between these three elements, you will experiment with getting unstuck in one area by strengthening another.

CHOICE

The choice is yours. You get to exit the mud puddle that's keeping you stuck and stop making excuses for why you can't get out by taking just a few baby steps toward a healthier you. It's not overwhelming or daunting if you just take it slowly. Just take a small step, stay in the moment, be patient with the results, and reassess before you take another small step. Along the way, you'll continue to ask, So now what?

In this book, I'll help you identify what's keeping you stuck, reveal the problems it causes, discuss how it's possible to change, and show you how to do it. You are worth it and can get this done. By not taking action, all of humanity suffers because you are an important and crucial part of many lives.

The choice is yours. Freedom awaits.

Section One

WHAT GETS US STUCK

We all get stuck and wander down the road of frustration, anger, disappointment, and general unhappiness. In this first section, we'll talk about the ways we get stuck. If you can identify where you're getting tripped up, you can avoid the experience entirely. If you're already stuck, that knowledge can help you understand how you got there. Self-awareness will save you lots of time pointing fingers at other people and things. It will also help determine your next step toward a stuck-free life.

One year, when I was in college, we got seventeen inches of snow overnight. My 1970 Chevy Nova was parked on the street in front of the house I rented. It took a long time to shovel the snow out from around the tires, but even afterward, I was still stuck.

So I enlisted a couple friends to help. In Minnesota, we learn the delicate skill of rocking our cars to get unstuck by trial and error. Push forward, then let it roll back, push again with some gas, and let it roll back. Each movement forward grabs a little more traction. If you get impatient and gun it too soon, the tires will spin, and the car won't move. You'll still be stuck.

We can be stuck in the mud, stuck with a pin, or stuck in traffic. We can also be stuck in a bad relationship, stuck trying to solve a problem, or stuck at a certain weight. We can be stuck on an idea, stuck in our job, or stuck because of what others think of us.

We can also be stuck in our life.

Stuck is a place where it feels impossible to move forward. Stuck is tolerating a bad marriage, fearing the future, or going through life without hope. Stuck is hitting the snooze button over and over because we don't want to get up and face the day. Stuck is being sick, sad, or skeptical.

BOILED LIKE A FROG

They say that if you put a frog in cold water and slowly bring it to a boil, he won't perceive any danger from the change that will eventually lead to his death.

This is what happened to me.

As a child, I thought stomachaches were normal. My mom's homegrown cucumbers soaked in salt water and onions caused stomach cramps, but oh boy did I love them! I would eat them until I was doubled over in pain.

My sisters and I were responsible for doing the dishes every night after dinner. It wasn't uncommon for me to be in the bathroom instead of the kitchen, cramped up in pain. My sisters would yell at me for trying to get out of doing the dishes—but honestly, I just had to curl up in a ball until the pain passed.

I also ate so much bread that it became a family joke. Butter or jelly wasn't necessary, just plain white bread. As a college student, I had a horrible diet. I ate candy bars, drank coffee, and consumed packaged meals on the run. The night my husband proposed to me, I had popcorn for dinner.

Pain in my stomach was a normal part of my life. My digestive system didn't work. But I didn't know this was out of the ordinary.

I was being boiled like a frog.

You must be saying to yourself, How in the world could you not know you were sick? Constant stomachaches? No regular relief in the bathroom? A diet of bread and popcorn? But it was true. The little irritations had turned into normal, everyday circumstances. My normal was unhealthy, and I didn't realize it could be different. I was stuck.

It could be the same with you. Nagging aches can seem normal if you get used to them. Negative thoughts that constantly drag down your attitude can be typical. Going through a day without being grateful for one thing may be commonplace. Any of us can be boiled like the frog, in regards to our body, our mind, or our spirit.

It's like a sliver. It hurts when you get it, but it will hurt more if we let it stay there, irritating the skin and getting infected. It must be removed . . . and it hurts.

Our lives are full of these slivers. We are stuck with anger, stuck with fear, stuck blaming others, or stuck living as an imposter to please people. When we learn how to remove those things, even though the process may be painful, we will no longer be stuck.

When I was depressed, I didn't understand all the factors that were contributing to my disease. Once exposed, there was something to work on to make things better. It's the same with any of our ails. Understanding the reasons we get stuck will help us see what needs to change and will reveal solutions.

There are three main reasons we get stuck: we're sick, sad, and skeptical. All three, however, can be improved and get us out of the metaphoric mud puddle we're sitting in.

In the first case, sickness, our compromised health makes us unable to take care of the challenges that come into our lives. Many of us are stuck in unhealthy bodies. We're overweight, inflexible, chronically tired, and inactive. We've grown accustomed to aches and pains and believe there's nothing to be done about it. We have trouble focusing and don't realize it's because our bodies aren't being cared for. We've got a million reasons that we *can't*, when most likely it's because we *won't*.

And when we take these steps, we will no longer be stuck.

The second reason we're stuck is sadness. We're not connected to one another. We're busier and busier and have easy access to technology twenty-four hours a day. We have fewer face-to-face conversations; our culture has become polarized and hatred is accepted; and we fear rejection so much that we allow things into our lives that aren't good for us. All these things cause our relationship skills to suffer.

We have more mental health issues than ever before. School shootings, fractured marriages, bullying, and suicide show just how much we, our children, and our society are struggling.

A third reason we're stuck is skepticism. We've lost our connection to the universe. I call it God—you can call it whatever you want. Organized religion has disappointed many of us. In response, we've figuratively thrown out the baby with the bathwater and want nothing to do with spirituality at all.

Where does all this sickness, sadness, and skepticism stem from? Let's look at the main sources. As we face these culprits, the way to freedom will become clear.

Chapter One
FEAR

I'm an expert on fear. Until ten years ago, it ruled my life. Besides normal fears of being rejected, public speaking, and death, I experienced gut-wrenching terror, panic attacks, and constant anxiety. Fear had me backed into a corner. It held me captive. What existed only in my mind defined my entire life. Fear was my continuous antagonist.

It seems I was born fearful and didn't need any horrible event to teach me how to fear the worst. My glass was half empty, people were out to get me, and good things would not come my way. It took a toll on my body, mind, and spirit.

Fear sets up barriers to keep us from harm. That's all fine and good, except that we've allowed fear to take charge and get way out of hand. In an effort to avoid all discomfort, we also avoid opportunities, growth, and joy. We go to the same awful place in our minds when someone looks at us sideways as if our long-time friend said they never want to see us again. The same gut-wrenching fight-or-flight sensation in our belly that should be reserved for real danger takes over our body even when no harm exists.

Fear will get us stuck too. It can be powerful if we let it. But it's just hyperbole. Like the drama queen in high school, fear makes a big deal about all kinds of things that aren't big deals at all. She's full of hot air and just trying to get attention. More often than not, our fears are a set of low-probability outcomes we have blown out of proportion and convinced ourselves are inevitable.

Imagine you meet a person who you're a little unsure of. You can just about hear the drama queen's warning, can't you? *Oh, he's the worst! Did you see the way he looked at you? Stay away from that loser! I heard . . .* But the drama queen could be wrong, and if you listen to her, you'll never get to find out if he's a loser or a prince. You easily take her fear, make it your own, build a wall, and keep opportunity out.

When we follow the drama queen and accept the fear, it's difficult to get beyond it. We become reactive and suspicious, just like her. We begin to eat a steady diet of fear, not even needing the drama queen to fabricate danger. We sit in front of the TV or listen to the news, filling our minds with images of dead bodies in war-torn countries, mug shots of people arrested for unspeakable crimes, and the most innocuous details of unusual happenings.

And, like junk food, it's bad for us.

The drama queen isn't easy to live with. She takes a toll on our body, our mind, and our heart. We grow exhausted, hunched over in a defensive position with our hands up and our eyes on full alert, just waiting for some catastrophe to happen. Our mind swirls with negative images and strategies to avoid pain. Our heart gets weighed down by sadness, hopelessness, and pessimism.

Fear also makes *us* hard to live with. We pull others into our vortex of fear, just like our mentor, the drama queen, has done. We annoy others with predictions of statistically unlikely events. We're gloomy and weak.

Fear has the power to direct our lives toward a small little corner. It's confining. Instead of offering freedom, it suspects a boogeyman around every corner. Nothing is safe, so why venture out? Fear leads us to believe there are bad consequences to every situation, so we limit our activities, attitudes, and hope. When we live in fear, our world gets small.

Fear wears us down. It changes who we are. It holds us captive. Have you ever made up scary stories in your mind about what might happen and felt the terror in your gut? Have you ever had pretend arguments in your mind to be prepared for the worst possible outcome? If so, you experienced negative consequences—even though most of what you feared would never come true. The damage was done.

Fear causes us to limit our experiences. We don't consider traveling overseas because the plane could crash over the ocean. We don't change jobs because we might dislike the new one even more than we do our current position. We aren't curious about what we don't know because it may make us uncomfortable.

We're prisoners.

Until I started calling fear out on her dirty deeds, she had immense power over my life.

Once I began to live in the present beautiful moment instead of the dreaded illusionary one, I quit wasting time and energy thinking about bad stuff that would never come true. Once I realized my value instead of being afraid I wasn't as good as the next person, I was free to live the life I was created for.

When you take a good look at where you're stuck, fear is probably at the core.

Ask yourself what you're afraid of. Read each one of the following statements slowly and ask yourself what fear is at the root. Keep asking yourself why until you get to the truth underlying the statement.

I'm afraid of failure.

I'm afraid of what other people will say.

I'm afraid I'm not enough.

I'm afraid of rejection.

I'm afraid people will leave if they know the real me.

I'm afraid of being wrong.

I'm afraid of making things worse.

I'm afraid of the unknown.

I'm afraid of change.

What are you really afraid of?

It's really important for you to stop now and ponder these fears. Ask yourself questions, and get honest in your heart and mind. Go to the root. This is where you'll begin to find freedom.

Let's look at some of the most common fears. When you begin to see yourself in these, you will have turned the corner toward freedom. Fear doesn't need to be your guide. Once you see what it is, it's not that difficult to call it out and move courageously forward. But without knowing what has you paralyzed, you are powerless to make a change.

The first two types of fear I'll discuss are external. They have to do with what we fear we will look like to others. We fear failure and having others mock us, and we fear being wrong and being judged by others. When we allow these fears to rule our lives, we get and stay stuck.

FEAR OF FAILURE

Atychiphobia. It's an irrational and persistent fear of failing. Fear of failure will get you stuck.

News flash—everyone fails. Even you. It may be uncomfortable, but it's a common human experience. It's not out of the ordinary or avoidable. To get better at anything, you must do it, and fail at it, over and over until you get it right.

If you ever took piano lessons, you know it's normal to hit the wrong key and play with the wrong timing. Your teacher probably had tons of patience as you fumbled around, struggling to make beautiful sounds. It takes time to practice. Lots of it. This is the normal process. Everyone must go through it.

But when I played piano, I didn't want to practice. I just wanted to be good. All the concentrating was hard, and it seemed like I would never improve. Who wants to sit down every day and be reminded of how far they have to go? I didn't like to hear my failure.

So I quit.

And, like tens of thousands of adults, I regretted giving up piano. Failure was part of the process, and I wasn't comfortable with it.

Remember the first time you talked to someone you thought was cute? Awkward, right? It was new, and you probably weren't good at it. After failing and realizing you wouldn't die, you stopped being afraid and got better. Aren't you glad you did?

It was hard, as children, to see that failure was actually our teacher and not our enemy. And the truth is that it's hard for adults too.

So, because failure is necessary to getting better, the first thing to get good at is failure. The first step to improving your life is to embrace your foibles, failings, and frailties.

Jeff Bezos, the founder of Amazon, said a smart person isn't someone who is always right. When hiring, he looks for people who can admit they are wrong—who can fail—and change their opinions often. Bezos has "observed that the smartest people are constantly revising their understanding and reconsidering a problem they thought they'd already solved. They're open to new points of view, new information, new ideas, contradictions, and challenges to their own way of thinking."

I'd be happy to be hired by Jeff Bezos. But he's not the only one who's figured this out. Scientific experiments benefit from failure. As a hypothesis is tested, experimental failures are used to determine the prediction is incorrect and guide the next steps toward a new hypothesis. And here's the most important and useful point: it's almost never a smooth and accelerating progression toward a fixed goal.

The fear of failure causes us to try protecting ourselves from the very thing that will make our lives better. The fear of failure isn't protecting you—it's limiting you. It doesn't protect your life but only limits the possibilities. And so you're stuck living in a place filled with excuses and fear.

Freedom comes when you're willing to fail until you succeed.

What are you afraid to fail at?

I began asking a very useful question to help me face my fear of failure: What's the worst thing that could happen?

Nine times out of ten, the worst thing is so far-fetched that it's laughable. Just speaking it out loud helps the bad thing lose its power. Usually, even if a bad thing is out there, it's still worth the risk.

I asked people what their worst fear would be if they had to get up in front of a crowd of a thousand people and talk about themselves. These are some of the answers they gave:

I could stumble over my words!

People might reject me.

I might say something stupid!

I might forget what to say.

I might talk too fast.

I might tell a joke and have no one laugh.

They might not listen.

I might freeze and not be able to talk.

My fly might be open.

I might wet my pants.

None of these are fatal. Most happen all the time as we talk to people one-on-one. We stumble over our words, people reject us, we say stupid things, we lose our train of thought, we talk too fast, we tell a joke and it flops, and our audience isn't listening (more than you know!). Even the rarest scenario, wetting your pants, is not death. Failure isn't terminal, it's just a little embarrassing. And we must go through failure on our way to success.

What are you gaining by
holding onto a fear of failure?

What are you losing by
holding onto a fear of failure?

The fear of failure keeps us stuck and will not allow the freedom we want in our lives. Next, we'll tackle another external fear—the fear of being wrong.

When we understand what is holding us back, we'll easily set these fears aside in favor of freedom to be and do more.

FEAR OF BEING WRONG

Foot-in-mouth disease: Have you had it? Have you asked a woman with a large belly when she was due, only to have her respond that she wasn't pregnant? Have you ever told someone the year you graduated from high school, as if to make a connection, and had them say they graduated *waaaayyy* later than you? I once saw a friend, flustered by a man's good looks, offer congratulations to him *at his father's funeral.*

Oops.

Although none of us want to be wrong, all of us sometimes are. It's part of being human.

But when the normal mistakes of life become so frightening that they stop us from being ourselves, we're prone to getting stuck. The fear of being wrong takes precedence, and we walk on eggshells to avoid looking silly. Being unable to accept our weakness makes us weak.

To avoid the agony of being wrong, we can sit back on the sidelines of life. When we refuse to participate, we won't be criticized for being a loudmouth or know-it-all, but we also won't be part of the solution.

Once, my husband and I had differing opinions about a business matter. He was sure the anticipated series of events would turn out one way, and I was equally convinced they would turn out another. We debated it over and over.

At the end of the day, it turned out I had been 100 percent wrong and he had been 100 percent right. It took me days to get over it. Then the lesson settled in. Instead of beating myself up for being wrong one time, I realized anyone could be 100 percent wrong, no matter how strong, smart, well-intentioned, or wise we are. It simply happens. No shame.

What are you afraid of being wrong about?

Picking the wrong salad dressing is a mistake, but no one dies or goes to prison. Choosing to drink and drive can be disastrous. We'll all be wrong at some time or another; it's just a matter of when and to what degree.

When we don't want to be wrong, we play small. We don't offer our opinions or add to problem-solving. We hold information to ourselves because stepping out and sharing it may make us feel ridiculous. Not wanting to appear mistaken causes us to hold ourselves back.

But everyone has a unique perspective. Is it fear that stops you from offering yours? You can't be wrong if you just offer your opinion. You also can't be wrong if you're sharing your experience. You were there, for goodness's sake!

The trouble with not sharing because we don't want to be wrong is that sometimes we're the only one who's 100 percent right. Withholding information out of fear may impact others negatively. And, on the flip side, sharing our perspective may impact others in a beautiful way.

The day before I ran the Boston Marathon in 2018, the weather forecast was dire. The winds were going to be blowing at twenty-five miles per hour, and heavy rains were predicted. An acquaintance of mine—a former yoga instructor with whom I only exchange Facebook likes—sent me a message about running in the wind. She could have been afraid of how it would come across. Would she appear to know more about running than I did? Would she be afraid of looking presumptuous? Would she be crossing a boundary because we weren't that close?

But she didn't think any of those things. She sent along information that was extremely helpful. It gave me critical information on how to run in the wind. I was helped dramatically through those grueling 26.2 miles because of the information she shared. Because she wasn't afraid of being wrong, she changed my race and, in some respects, even changed my life.

The fear of being wrong begs the question, Why do we expect to always be right? It's a good one to ponder. We must go after the source of our discomfort to avoid this fear. Thinking it through will certainly cause the impossible standard to dissipate. Then we will walk in the freedom we all desire.

Why do you expect to always be right?

The next two fears—caring too much about what others think and the fear of being ourselves—are internal. What others think of us is in their own minds, and we may never know even if we ask. When we're afraid of showing our true self, we cannot know how people would respond if we did.

Caring Too Much What Others Think

I was afraid they would think I wasn't cool and reject me. To make sure this didn't happen, I did what they did, laughed when they laughed, and followed the cool kids. The struggle was real . . . in junior high.

High school got even worse. Afraid I wasn't enough and that I'd be alone, I did all I could to fit in. The stakes were higher, but the risk was worth it. Being labeled a dork or not being invited to parties had me doing all kinds of crazy stuff. I cared *too much* about what others thought of me, and it got me stuck.

Most of us care to some degree about what others think of us. It's normal to want positive feedback. The question is, how much power does it have? If we hear a negative reaction, do we quickly respond and fall back in line? How does the fear of what others may think affect our behavior?

Many of us have had situations where we were humiliated because of something we said or did. We made a mistake, failed at something, or blurted out something stupid. We got a bad reaction, and it was painful.

So we worked very hard to make sure it would never happen again. Our motivation to avoid pain overtook our desire to be authentic. "If I just pretend I like what they like," we reason with ourselves, "they'll believe I do. They'll like me, and I won't be rejected."

We get good at pretending. Our authentic self fades away. Often, we don't even know who we truly are anymore. We say things like, "I don't know what I'd like to do with my life," and, "I don't care what we do." Our life becomes directed by our fear of pain instead of an acceptance of our self. We're so afraid of being judged by others that we forget who we are.

If we aren't careful, trying to please others at our own expense becomes a habit. We automatically limit our thinking to what we think others will accept. Soon, anyone we come in contact with has the power to change the direction of our life.

When we weigh everyone's comments the same, we're prone to getting stuck, sad, or confused. If instead, we first pay attention to *who* is giving us a comment and not *what* is actually said, we'll be less likely to accept bad information or ignore useful comments.

We can care too much about what others think of us when we don't feel good about ourselves. Instead of knowing who we are and recognizing our strengths and weaknesses, we look for validation from those around us. The problem is that the validation is fickle.

Who are you listening to?

Are you allowing strangers to determine your worth? Are you listening carefully to correction from those who love you? Whose voice speaks the loudest in your mind?

If you find yourself thinking, "Oh, that's me! I'm awful! I let everyone change my mind!" you're not alone. It's a common experience that can be changed by recognizing how destructive it is. We just need to begin listening to ourselves more than others to direct the actions in our lives.

Our lives are like a theatre production. Who is the director of your life? Is it your spouse? Your boss? Your kids? Your friends? The guy at the gas station? Is it the salesperson at the mall, the driver who cut you off in traffic, or the telemarketer who won't leave you alone? Are they telling you to walk across the stage slowly when you want to dance in circles?

Why do you care what they say?

Freedom comes when we fire the director, even if they're loud and obnoxious, and sit in the director's chair. No one ought to have that position except you.

Our fears can be so powerful that they cause us to do crazy things. We're driven by other people's thoughts instead of our own. The fear of being wrong in another's eyes, regardless of who they are, has us chasing an elusive legitimacy.

And we're stuck. Using other people's opinions as our guide leads us in the wrong direction. It's only when we take responsibility for our thoughts and actions that we get unstuck. We can learn to trust ourselves for the direction of our life.

FEAR OF AUTHENTICITY

The fear of being authentic leads us to being . . . inauthentic.

The world needs *you*. It needs the authentic, unedited, raw version of you.

Why do you want to be someone else?

Besides, you aren't very good at being someone else's version of you.

I lip-synched "Straighten Up and Fly Right" with my girl-friend in the eighth-grade talent show. It's as close as I've come to stardom. Although I would love to be a singer, I wouldn't make a very good Beyoncé. And she wouldn't be a very good me. I don't have her talent, and she doesn't have mine.

Typically, we're not trying to be rock stars—but we can get stuck trying to be like our friends, to be the life of the party, or to fulfill the expectations of others. It's a tough way to live, constantly trying to be something we're not. It's mentally and emotionally exhausting. And we're stuck.

When we pretend to be someone else, we leave the people in our lives unsure about who we really are. Imagine you live with someone who really loves to be outdoors but forces themselves to stay inside and read a book because they think that's what you want them to do. You're clueless about their desire to go hike in the mountains. They get grouchier and grouchier, and you have no idea what's going on. You wonder why they're so sullen and agitated.

Finally, they explode and say, "I gotta get out of here! I have to go hiking!"

You wait one second, blink, and then ask, "Why didn't you ever tell me you wanted to go hiking?"

They yell back at you, "Because you wouldn't like it!"

This is a silly example, but being someone you *think* someone else wants you to be doesn't work. When we hide behind what we think others want out of the fear of showing who we are, no one wins.

COPYCAT

Joyce and I became fast friends. She had a flair for life and was fun and energetic. Her extroverted personality was a great complement to my quieter nature.

She insisted I decorate my house, so I did. She explained the benefits of decorator pillows, so I bought dozens of them. She wallpapered every square inch of her house, so I did too.

I began to act like Joyce instead of myself. On a visit to my hometown, I explained my new painting technique, which brought curious glances from my sisters. "You did what?" they asked.

"I used a toilet bowl brush to paint black streaks on my dining room wall," I said, as if this were the most ordinary thing in the world because it was what Joyce did. When I heard myself saying it out loud, I remember thinking, *Wait . . . is that normal?*

There was plenty to admire about Joyce, but I was trying to be her instead of me. I let Joyce have power over me. She could have asked me to dress in a sheet, put a garland on my head, and go to a party, and I would have done it. I let her love for decorating become my own, but I didn't love it as much as her. I gave up myself to be her friend.

When I was miniature Joyce, I was forgetting about myself. I like to take walks and talk about deep subjects, but Joyce wasn't into that. Afraid I wouldn't have friends, I stopped being who I was and became what I thought she wanted me to be. Neither one of us benefited from the arrangement, and I was stuck pretending to be someone I wasn't.

We pretend all kinds of things in order to be accepted. This leads to all kinds of confusion. We get stuck when we do what we think others want us to do instead of doing what comes naturally to us. Our thoughts are wrapped up in assuming what others are thinking about us. In our attempt to not be rejected, we turn into a person we think they want instead of who we are. Now we're both confused.

We do what we think others want us to do—but they don't want us to do it at all. They want us to be ourselves.

Who are you pretending to be?

When I was depressed, no one knew it. I was such a good imposter that people simply saw me as a moody, driven, reactive overachiever who was cold and distant. It couldn't have been further from the truth. I was insecure, sad, and trying to prove my worth by doing things well. I wanted desperately to have friends but was afraid that if they knew the real me, they'd run for the hills.

Ultimately, people want the authentic, true version of us. We are free when we're authentic, and this lets everyone we interact with be free too. Freedom is not thinking about what you think others want from you. Freedom is being loved for who you truly are.

We can be afraid to be authentic because we don't believe we're enough. Many people look at other people, compare themselves, and decide the other person is enough but they are not. As we look at what they have, we focus on what we don't. Comparison gets us stuck.

Believing we're not enough is like stopping the natural swinging of a pendulum.

What would it take for you to know you're enough and be free?

THE PENDULUM

Relationships are like a pendulum. We stand face to face, toe to toe. One person leans forward, expressing their wishes, forcing the other to lean back; the other person then pushes back with what they are willing to accommodate and what they aren't. The pendulum keeps swinging until the tension is resolved and both stand upright.

As two people are in this swaying movement, they each take a turn feeling weak and unsteady as they bend backward to accommodate the other. It may feel like the only thing to do to keep the relationship alive is to stay bent over backward, pretending we are comfortable, because to push against the opposing force and hold our ground is scary. What if they walk away?

When we stop being authentic, the pendulum will lean to one side, becoming unbalanced as we lean backward. We leave the other person in the dark as to who we are and what we want. We allow one person to dictate the position of the pendulum, and the relationship suffers.

But if each person honors themselves while also accepting the other where they are at, the swings become less pronounced. This is beautiful and healthy. Neither fears being authentic, and each accepts the true and honest version of the other. As each of them shows their true nature, the other can respond without pushing or leaning.

In a healthy exchange, we come to rest where neither of us is leaning backward or forward. This requires being authentic and honest.

Hopefully, you are beginning to see what a powerful and deceptive motivator fear is. We can't follow our fears of failure, being wrong, what others think, and being authentic without getting stuck.

The last area where fear takes its nasty toll is our fear of making things worse. We either fear what we do will make things worse for ourselves or are afraid of the unknown.

FEAR OF MAKING THINGS WORSE

Like a knight in shining armor, fear's motive is to protect. But he's a noxious tower of metal, and I hope you're beginning to understand how limiting he is.

When we're afraid of making things worse, ironically, we make things worse. Staying static is no solution. We must act.

There are many reasons we don't attempt to change things. But we know that if we don't try something new, we're guaranteed to keep things as they are. We won't know whether things will get better or worse until we take a step toward change. When the fear of making things worse takes over, we're bound to get stuck.

When I was depressed, my low self-worth and belief others knew more than me kept me from taking a step to make things better. I believed my ideas could only make things worse, not better. I was afraid to rock the boat. I felt I couldn't ask for what I wanted. I was afraid it could make the relationship worse. I didn't want to offer my opinion because it could cause conflict.

We can all be afraid to take steps to get unstuck because we're afraid that, if we do what it takes to get out, we'll make it worse. Instead of getting through the maze, we will need to go back to the place we took the wrong turn and go the other way.

But the fear of making things worse is unwarranted and un-tested. It keeps us from solutions, risks, and both success and failure. The fear of making things worse is unhealthy because, as we discussed in the section on the fear of failure, we need to try new things to get unstuck.

What are you afraid will happen by taking a step?

FEAR OF THE UNKNOWN

No one knows what the future has in store. We hold tight to things the way they are out of fear that change will bring about circumstances we don't know how to deal with. We can stay stuck because we cannot predict the future.

It's easier to go about our day the same way we went about yesterday. It's easier to take the same way to work, hang out with the same people, and watch the same TV shows. It's easier to put up with her complaining than to express your feelings, to go along with his plans than to share your own, and to let your kids have what they want than to give them what they need.

What unknown event are you afraid of?

Often, we feel a desire to predict the future to avoid the un-known. We get stuck declaring what his reaction will be *because* we're afraid to face his actual reaction. We stop so much activity with statements like, "Well, he *always*," "She would *never*," or, "I *couldn't* do that!" We're in the fortune-telling business.

These declarations just protect us from the unknown. We stay stuck with what we *think* we know because we don't really want to know. It's circular. Changes in technology are making the inevitability of change even clearer. New options for managing our life are constantly appearing. When we learn to embrace the positive aspects of changes around us, we're more likely to adapt to the uncertain but inevitable changes which come our way.

THE SCANNER

Years ago, when the cutting edge of technology was the ability to change the fonts on our documents, pagers, and a fax machine, we purchased a new copy machine for our business. It had a few bells and whistles, but mostly it copied images in black and white on one piece of paper at a relatively fast speed. As the office equipment purchaser, fixer, toner czar, and strategizer—just a few of my many hats—I decided that was all we needed.

At the time, I wasn't one to fix something that wasn't broken. Continually watching the dollars so we would end up with a profit each year, I was shortsighted and, well . . . cheap.

Somewhere along the line, a friend told me he had purchased a scanner for his office and loved it. "What do you use it for?" I asked skeptically.

"Oh, I don't know," he replied. "I just sent my dad a recipe." That wasn't enough of a reason for me to buy a scanner.

About six months later, the copier salesman started talking about having a copier that could scan documents. Again, I asked, "What would I use it for?" to which he could not give me a good answer. Maybe he was a bad salesman, or maybe he knew I'd say no regardless of what he said. *Why change what I know is working?* I thought. I held the notion the future would always be the same as the present.

Over a year later, a new copier salesman came to our door. He said, "I don't know how you run your business with this machine," referring to my faithful copier (which, by the way, was paid for). That made me mad. He was implying I didn't know how to run a business. *Of course I know how to run a business*, I thought. *I have one, don't I?*

But maybe I wasn't running the business *well*.

Before long, I purchased a new copier. By this time, a scanner came standard with a purchase because it was so often used. *Oh well*, I thought sarcastically. *If I ever want to send my Dad a recipe, I'll be ready.*

And then we began to scan documents. They magically appeared in a special "Scanned Doc" folder, and we could pull them into emails and whisk them away over the internet. Almost overnight, I was scanning almost everything and copying almost nothing. Our postage went down as we sent electronic files instead of snail mail. We used less paper and saved storage space. It was unbelievable!

Why had I missed out on this new opportunity for so long? Because I was afraid of the unknown. You can call it pride. You can call it being unnecessarily thrifty (or cheap). You can call it ignorance. You can call it stubbornness. I call it all those things. It was one of the best lessons I ever learned.

I was stuck in my old way of thinking because I was afraid of trying something new. This led to skepticism and barriers. It stopped me from considering new possibilities.

We can all fall into using our fear of the unknown and getting stuck. The sure thing seems to be the safer bet. At least it's known. It takes courage to try something new, and it may feel vulnerable and risky. To avoid the discomfort, we form a habit of not trying anything new. This habit ensures we will be stuck.

SUMMARY

There are so many things to be afraid of, but hardly any of them will ever come true. We spend time fearing things that cannot harm us and miss out on opportunities right in front of our faces. We can never get back the time that we spent fretting over a potential problem that never came to be. We lose out on friendships, successes, lessons, and simply being ourselves.

Fear isn't a good motivator. Fear keeps us trapped. Fear causes us to shut down. Fear focuses on scarcity. Fear focuses only on the self. Fear is defensive. Fear keeps us stuck.

Fear is our enemy.

Chapter Two

FEELINGS

As if our fears were not enough to stop us dead in our tracks, we can also be unable to move forward in life because of all the rest of our feelings. Our emotions are powerful. They affect not only our thoughts but also our bodies. They can cause us to slip into the mud puddle before we even know it.

What is it with those dang emotions?

When I was depressed, I bemoaned emotions altogether. They seemed to cause me nothing but trouble. I felt everyone's suffering on top of my own. The plight of those trapped by poverty, my friend's recent dilemma, and our children's unhappiness all landed squarely in my heart. I felt everything so deeply. It was exhausting. It seemed all emotions did was cause me pain.

I discovered that my feelings were a signal of something inside me needing adjustment. My anger could reveal insecurity or hurt. Although I thought sadness showed my capacity for empathy, it actually revealed weaknesses, wrong mindsets, and disappointments. It was so hard to see how many adjustments I needed to make. But this new knowledge was enlightening because it helped me figure out how my feelings could help direct my life.

Some very wise teaching revealed my feelings were my responsibility. All my life, I had believed others could "make" me feel a certain way, and it was their fault when I felt bad. Each day I went from feeling good to bad based on how I perceived everybody else. It felt like I was a pinball, bouncing off all those around me. This had me stuck.

Let's look at some of the ways our feelings get us stuck. If you see yourself in these words, know this understanding will bring you freedom. Much of the battle comes from identifying *what* has you stuck. Once you've peeked behind the curtain and seen what's there, it's really not that hard to change. Without this knowledge, however, you'll stay stuck.

The first reason our feelings get in our way has to do with others. I know these feelings well because they ruled my life for many years. We blame our feelings on them.

BLAMING OTHERS

When we blame other people for our troubles, we get stuck letting them decide when we'll solve them.

I could write a whole book on how I have blamed other people for my problems. In an effort to avoid painful feelings, I threw blame onto someone else. But the pain didn't go away with blame, so I stayed stuck.

The blame game is easy because there are so many people to blame for our problems.

I'm overweight because my husband wants to eat meat and potatoes every night!

I'm stressed out because the neighbor is so loud!

I don't get paid enough because no one around here notices how much I do!

I'm unhappy because my friends are such jerks!

I'm depressed because . . . my mom was depressed, my dad was anxious, I'm a woman, my husband has big dreams, my kids won't behave, I can't find coconut milk in the grocery store, no one understands me, women are mean, I have bad genes, my eyes are crossed, I have a stupid brother, we don't always agree, my church isn't perfect, he made me cry . . . blah, blah, blah.

It kept me stuck for years.

Blame is easy but unproductive. We use it as an exclamation point to our problems. *See! There! It's because he . . . !* Although it may feel good in the moment, this blame gets us nowhere but stuck. We throw the ball into someone else's court, but we're the one who still has the problem.

Who or what are you blaming for your most difficult problem?

BUSY HUSBAND

My husband and I got married in our midtwenties. Like most young couples, we imagined our lives full of understanding and acceptance. Although our families were similar, striking differences were just below the surface and began to show themselves immediately.

I think we were courageous to marry one another. We walked down the aisle, unconsciously knowing that we needed each other to be full and complete. Mike's spontaneity was so attractive when we dated but then grew to irritate me, and it took on the word *irresponsible*. He loved my loyalty and passion, but those turned into the annoying habits of inflexibility and stubbornness.

Early in our marriage, Mike would work long hours and then stop by the golf course to practice on his way home. I pleaded with him to spend more time together, but his independence was being suffocated by marriage. Instead of letting him have time alone, I pushed harder and sparks flew.

We had children and started a business. Mike continued to sneak out early and play golf while I took care of the business, kids, and home. I was stuck blaming my unhappiness on him instead of letting him know I wanted things to change. Golf became his mistress. She didn't demand anything of him. I hated her. Why didn't he love me . . . the nagging, insecure, demanding, unhappy spouse?

We were stuck because we blamed each other for what was happening. It was easier than looking at ourselves.

I blamed him for not spending enough time together, and he blamed me for being so needy. The truth was I wanted attention from him, and he wanted time to himself. We needed to share what we wanted instead of blaming each other for what we didn't have.

Eventually we learned to communicate what we wanted instead of blaming each other for what we lacked. The blame had us stuck waiting for the other person to change. Taking ownership of our needs got us unstuck.

No problem was ever solved by finding out whose fault it was. The feelings that go along with our problems are a signal for us to own them and figure out a solution. When those feelings turn into blame, we will definitely be stuck.

YOUR FEELINGS BECOME MY FEELINGS

The motivational speaker Jim Rohn famously said we are the average of the five people we spend the most time with. Who we spend time with and how we relate to them affects our life in a big way. When we hang out with people who are sick, sad, or skeptical, our feelings will become gloomy too. Unless we are strong physically, mentally, and spiritually, we will adopt the feelings of those around us.

Because of this principle, we can be unaware of how sick we are because those around us are also sick. Our friends become an unofficial measure of what it means to feel good. They are twenty pounds overweight, so our ten pounds don't seem so bad. They pooh-pooh exercise, so our walk around the block a couple of times a week seems fit. And their complaints about how busy they are and how little sleep they get push us to do more and sleep less.

It makes sense that some of our friends have the same weaknesses we do. The same stuck-ness. We find comfort in someone else understanding our failings. But we can stay stuck if those around us want us to stay there. As social beings, we're vested in the tribe. When someone within the group takes an unexpected action, it causes the rest to compare this new behavior with their own.

When someone in the clan chooses to be healthy, the others will seek to bring them back into the group's standard of health because they don't like to feel uncomfortable with change. Ever tried to start a diet and then go to dinner with friends? If you decide not to have dessert, they make comments like, "A little chocolate cake won't kill ya," "Just take a little bite," or "You gotta live!"

There's pressure to conform with the group.

In general, I don't drink alcohol. It puts me to sleep and gives me headaches. My behavior has nothing to do with what anyone else does. Just like I like to wear red, I don't judge others who don't wear red. Simple as that.

There are many occasions to drink alcohol in our society. If someone invites you to happy hour, you're not obligated to drink alcohol, but those who are drinking might put pressure on you to help themselves feel comfortable with their own drinking.

The pressure to conform can be difficult to handle because not conforming can reduce the number of happy hours you're invited to. We're forced to be authentic and be left outside the social group or play along and keep being invited.

It can be a lonely transition if you've been pretending to be someone you're not. Some people go their whole life not letting other people know who they truly are. They are stuck.

In a healthy society, people celebrate each other's differences and allow each person to express themselves uniquely. In an unhealthy group, we often fall back into line and stop thinking about how we could become better, more authentic, or stronger. Our fear of being rejected by our people keeps us stuck.

Our friendships may draw us back into being stuck because they're stuck too. If you choose your friends because they have the same stuck behaviors as you, you're at risk of staying in that same stuck place for life.

There is so much power in accountability. To maintain a healthy weight, remain active, or value our sleep, we must rub shoulders with those who value these attributes. Conversations will revolve around healthy recipes or hearing about the latest fitness class. The groupthink does not brag about their lack of sleep and overindulgence in work. We feel supported and free.

An obesity study done at Harvard concluded our eating habits are affected by not only our friends but also our friends' friends. Even our friends' friends' friends impact what and how much we eat. People we don't even know are affecting how we live our lives. These social networks are powerful predictors of our behavior.

OVERCOMING DIABETES

There was a congregation that met every Sunday for a church-sponsored meal. Not only were people able to have lunch, but breaking bread together helped the churchgoers form a stronger community. The meals consisted of fried chicken, creamed corn, white bread, juice, and pie. The problem was that this meal was very unhealthy because a large portion of the congregation suffered from diabetes.

As they ate together each week, they supported each other's unhealthy eating habits. Although those with diabetes had been told by doctors to avoid these foods, they found support at these meals from others who were sick. Their social bonds were held together with unhealthy food choices. The group supported stagnation instead of the change most of them needed to make because of their illness.

Fortunately, the congregation recognized this problem and changed what they ate to healthier options. As a group, they moved in a healthy direction. Their health improved and they continued to be in a tight-knit community.

Which behaviors have you adopted because they're what your friends want you to do?

Belonging to a group of people who shun healthy living is a good indication of your future health. But this is much further reaching than just physical health. We can also be stuck because we take on the unhealthy mental characteristics of our friends.

Those with weak mental health skills speak poorly of others, don't like themselves, and lack boundaries. When things go wrong, they find other people are to blame. Emotions are difficult for them to control. When we spend a lot of our time with people with weak mental health skills, we are likely to take on their countenance.

THE INTERNSHIP

When I was in college, I had an accounting internship with a large retailer. It was my initiation into the real world of business. I worked as a support to the internal auditors and accounts payable.

It was so exciting to drive up to the ginormous building on my first day. It had a cafeteria and walking trails along a pond in the back. I was ushered through a sea of cubicles and assigned one of my own. The internal auditors were cool women in their twenties. They wore hip clothes and traveled a great deal of the time. I hoped I could become one of them someday.

As I settled into my role, I was asked to go to lunch with some women from accounts payable. The unofficial leader of the group was a pregnant woman in her thirties whom I'll call Marcia. Just like girls in junior high, Marcia's group faithfully followed her to the cafeteria when she decided it was time for lunch, listened to her talk most of the lunch hour, and followed her back to their cubicles.

She was a mean girl.

Since Marcia loved to talk about herself, I soon found out all about her. She lived in the suburbs with her husband and several children. According to her, the people in her life were awful, so she liked to go to a country-western bar every weekend without her husband and "have some fun."

One weekend, Marcia, the groupies, and I went with her to the bar and partied like college students. I was the only one who qualified as such but had long outgrown the desire to get drunk and foolish. Marcia thought it was okay to drink while she was pregnant. It was there, after a couple of cocktails, I heard her secret.

Marcia's baby was due in just a couple of months, but she wasn't sure who the father was. I looked around the table at some of the other women to see if this was really true. Sure as shootin', Marcia's life was complicated by this little detail, which would likely expose itself at the time of the birth.

I wasn't sure the "world of business" was all the promotional flyers at the business school had promised.

The rest of the summer went from bad to worse. The constant complaining each lunch hour about crappy people in Marcia's life became exhausting. I found other things to do at lunch. My knowledge about accounting increased, but the internship taught me more about the power of a negative person.

Marcia was stuck with unhealthy thinking. She was mean to those around her and sought to control them. She was in the habit of lying to her husband about where she went. Her life was spinning out of control. Unfortunately for the women who followed her, these bad habits were infiltrating their thinking too.

Marcia was also stuck in an unhealthy body. Even though social drinking while pregnant wasn't frowned upon then, getting drunk while pregnant certainly was. And her confession of not knowing who the father of her child was showed unhealthy sexual behaviors putting her, her baby, and her partners at risk. I wondered what had happened to Marcia to get her to believe her body was so unimportant.

But most importantly, Marcia was stuck spiritually. Her life had no meaning. She was clearly unhappy and seemed to pour that same sentiment on those around her. I suspect her primary difficulty was the inability to love herself. In hindsight, I feel a lot of compassion for her.

Working with her for just a few months in the summer had a lasting impact on me. Her lack of hope about her life was terribly sad. Her constant complaining about her job left me wondering why she stayed. It seemed she had faith in nothing, not even herself. I was excited to get back to school so that I would no longer have to feel Marcia's unhealthy vibe. The stress of exams and no money was better than being sucked down into

Marcia's mud puddle. I never found out who the father was, and I remember very little about any of the other women.

Marcia's negativity taught me an important lesson: we get stuck when we hang out with negative people. When we hang out with people who are sick, sad, or skeptical, we're prone to take on their unhealthy habits.

The next two reasons our feelings can be problematic have to do with what we do with them inside our mind and heart. This internal dialogue creates disturbances. When we rely on our feelings to tell us the truth or allow the weight of them to make us feel powerlessness, we'll be stuck for sure. Only in our strength will we be free from these burdens.

RELYING ON OUR FEELINGS TO TELL US THE TRUTH

Feelings can be fickle and aren't typically a good anchor to hook our boat to. They ebb and flow based on the weather, how much sleep we've gotten, and our expectations. We need our mind and our wisdom to drive us. When we rely on our feelings for direction and truth, we're following the wrong leader. Like a kite that has lost its string, we float on the winds of emotion with no determined destination. One emotion leads to another, and soon we're lost.

Our feelings, however, are a powerful signal. Like a road sign, they point out *something*. What it is, however, will take more than our feelings to discern.

THE REAL ISSUE

Jodie was a woman known as a force. She was opinionated and pushy. She was also smart and got a lot of things done. For years, I disliked Jodie. She made her opinions known in loud, high-pitched tirades. I got to know her tactics well. She wasn't used to cooperating with others and instead acted like a bowling ball shattering the pins. She came from a family of privilege, wore expensive clothes, and had fake nails.

For years I argued with Jodie in my mind, calling her out on her shameful behavior and bringing her to her knees. In my fantasy conversations, I'd have the last word and she would have to leave corrected and ashamed. I blamed Jodie for how mad I was. I allowed my feelings about Jodie to keep me stuck. But it wasn't her. It was me.

It took years, but finally I got sick of how much time I spent thinking about how awful Jodie was. Thoughts of her were consuming more time in my mind than I cared to admit. I asked myself a simple question, "What is it that bugs you so much about Jodie?"

Quickly, I listed the reasons: She's obnoxious! She's self-centered! She's rude! She lies!

"Okay, Cathy . . . there are plenty of obnoxious, self-centered, rude liars in this world," I said to myself. "What is it about *her* that bugs you?"

I paused before I answered my own question. A little less certain, I continued with my litany of hate-filled accusations: "Men fear her! She's bad for our community! She's awful . . ."

Again, I asked myself the same question: "What is it about *her* that bugs you so much?"

I felt like I was slowly taking an elevator to the basement. It was quiet and dark, and I was getting real with myself. There was a reason down there, and I suspected it had nothing to do with Jodie. My feelings of anger had kept me stuck for years. It was finally dawning on me that I had the power to take care of these crazy thoughts and wasted time.

What was it? I paused and closed my eyes, understanding deep in my soul that the answer was there. I had to wait for it.

This reason didn't want to expose her ugly self. A dim light disclosed the very thing that had kept me stuck for years.

The reason was timid and afraid. She was sad to look at, and I felt compassion when I realized where she had come from. It had been so long I had forgotten she was there, giving life to my sadness that had turned to anger and resulted in being stuck.

The reason for my anger was that Jodie got attention from others, and I wanted that attention.

That was it. Very simple. All my negative emotions were just a way to keep the truth of the matter hidden. My desire for attention stemmed from childhood experiences I hadn't understood or dealt with. Years later, they were still wreaking havoc on my life, keeping me from moving forward.

My reaction to Jodie's behavior had actually been a clue. Like the blinking lights of a railroad crossing, my anger about Jodie was a sign something deep inside me had to be dealt with. There were questions I needed to answer and feelings I needed to accept.

But now that I recognized them, I was free.

When we believe our feelings are truth, we will stay stuck. They are simply a signal for something that needs changing within us.

What feelings are a signal in your life?
Where did they come from?

I've tested this out countless times since my breakthrough about Jodie. Every time I have a huge emotional reaction to something, stepping back to find out what it's revealing calms me down and brings understanding. My emotions have become my friends, and I trust them to point out something I can't consciously point to.

Our feelings come not only from our thoughts but from our body. When I run low on food, I get hangry. My body is like a toddler who screams out and makes demands whenever she's uncomfortable. She has her own voice. The great news is that when I realize my negative emotions are coming because I haven't had breakfast, I don't let my feelings run wild and ruin the rest of my day. I simply eat breakfast, and voilà—I feel good again.

Our spirit also reveals emotions. We can "feel" bad emotionally because our spiritual muscle is weak. When hope, gratitude, joy, and love aren't at the front of our thoughts, we're prone to allowing feelings of fear, thoughtlessness, unhappiness, and hatred rule the roost. Simply putting the spiritual principles into practice will turn our emotions from negative to positive in a split second. Hardly any effort required!

When we realize our feelings come from all these places, we are equipped to use them for our benefit.

FEELING POWERLESS TO CHANGE

Many of us feel powerless over our lives. We believe life is just how it is, and we're stuck living it a certain way. With this internal struggle, the possibility of change seems impossible. We feel there's nothing we can do to change our circumstances or the feelings that go along with them.

I understand.

THE BUSINESS

My husband and I started a business and felt stress at every turn. There were never enough hours in the day, and risks loomed large. I felt our children were getting the short end of the stick.

My frustration grew, and I felt powerless to change. I worried that if I stepped away from the business, no one would mind the till. Anxiety was my main motivator, sprinkled with a hefty dose of arrogance in the belief that things would not run as well without me.

A combination of not knowing what to do next along and a lack of confidence in my ability to create change had me drowning. I felt powerless. My husband needed me, my children needed me, and I was stuck.

Like a dog chasing its tail, I put my head down and faced each day, never looking up to see how it could be changed or improved. Exhausted and tired, my husband and I finally had a good heart-to-heart. We came up with the idea of hiring someone to help me. It meant change and risk. I fretted over what it would cost but knew I was at my limit.

The idea that we cannot change the circumstances of our life leaves us in a weak position. This feeling of powerlessness gets us stuck. Each one of us owns our life and has the potential to make a change. The choices may seem difficult, but they are easier than living without them.

What makes you feel powerless over your life?

SUMMARY

Our feelings can make us stuck. When we blame others for our emotions instead of taking responsibility for them, we are stuck. Because we will naturally adopt the attitudes and feelings of those we spend the most time with, hanging with an unhealthy crowd may make us stuck. The desire to belong to a group can make us stuck when we succumb to the pressure to conform to unhealthy habits. And, until we see our feelings as a sign something inside us needs fixing, we'll follow them down a path that will keep us stuck. Feelings are fickle yet ever present. They can serve as a signpost for change or lead us down a dead-end path. Finally, if we feel we are powerless to change, we will stay stuck waiting for others to solve our problems.

Chapter Three

BELIEFS

What do you believe about yourself? Are there conclusions you've drawn based on your age, gender, economic status, body build, heredity, or opportunities? Do you limit your dreams based on where you live, how much money you don't have, who you know, your grades in school, or past mistakes? Do you begin sentences with, "I'd *never . . .*" or "I can't . . ."? Do you have a pocketful of excuses ready to pull out to protect yourself?

In the book *Big Magic,* Elizabeth Gilbert talks about how many of us have suffered from the limiting beliefs put in our minds by others who thought it was a good idea to tell us how bad we were at something. We can live our whole life believing we are unathletic because Mr. Gym Teacher was having a bad day and pointed out an error at a particularly sensitive time in our life. Maybe a mean girl scoffed at your new haircut and so you never tried another new style again. Maybe it came from that pimply faced boyfriend who said you were fat just before he dumped you.

Our limiting beliefs get us stuck. To protect ourselves, we set up walls. Those walls are the limiting beliefs that keep us safe from risk. They don't allow us to ever create again. They keep us from believing we can get better. They keep us locked out of trying something new and expanding who we are. Here are some walls, or limiting beliefs, we set up:

Doing that would be selfish.

Don't draw attention to yourself.

If I fail, they'll be ashamed of me.

Succeeding will make my friends feel bad.

I'd feel guilty if I asked for that.

I'm afraid of being disappointed.

My mom would never have done that.

My dad wouldn't approve.

My husband would think that's weird.

These limiting beliefs given to us by others also keep us stuck.

You're too old!

You're a girl!

You're not smart enough!

You don't know anything about that!

You're not pretty enough!

You're too short!

You're too young!

You don't have enough experience!

Limiting beliefs can undo our progress. One time, my coach drew attention to my swimming stroke. Someone mocked me, and I felt ashamed. The voice in my head yelled, "Get back in line, Cathy! It's bad and arrogant to be good at something! Never again will you take a step to draw attention to yourself. Play small. Fit in. Quit being yourself."

We learned many limiting beliefs as children as we listened carefully to what adults said. We learned to obey and listen because we needed them to do things for us. Those parental voices can still speak loudly in our adult minds too, becoming limiting beliefs.

As we grow into adulthood, our beliefs need to grow too. We must question what we've been told and reframe our thinking to our truth. We get stuck when we fail to go through that process. The beliefs we have about ourselves will either move us forward or keep us stuck.

When I was depressed, I believed I was incompetent, unlovable, weak, destined for sadness, stupid, ugly, unholy, unworthy, unimportant, incapable, too fearful, too conservative, not fun enough, not acceptable, and not cool enough. Those limiting beliefs kept me stuck. They kept me from my strengths and from those around me. They boxed me in a cage.

When we challenge our limiting beliefs, we take a step toward freedom.

What are your limiting beliefs?

GENDERED BELIEFS

As women, we can make our voices smaller. It's hard for us to get our heads around thoughts such as "I'm a better athlete than he is," "I'm better at business than he is," or "I'm more able to make this difficult decision."

I had a friend who said she'd like to lose weight, but her husband didn't want to "eat like a rabbit." She believed her husband deserved to eat what he wanted, and she didn't. Isn't she entitled to say, "I don't want to eat like a caveman"? Who told her that becoming what he wanted her to become was better than being herself? Limiting beliefs. Unfortunately, he gets a boiled-down version of her and never gets the benefits of her full beauty.

There is always room for compromise. Each of you can "come to the table" with your requests and arrive at a solution.

What limiting beliefs do you have because of your gender?

WOMEN ONLY / MEN ONLY

Men stay stuck when they back away from doing things because their limiting beliefs cause them to be afraid of looking feminine. I know a man who boasts that he does not know how to cook and has never changed a diaper. Is it true he can analyze a complicated set of financial statements but can't figure out how to boil water or clean a baby's bottom? I don't think so.

It goes both ways. Women's limiting beliefs can see every fix-it job around the house as her mate's responsibility. He wasn't born with a hammer in his hand, and he's not less of a man because of it. There's also no male gene for being better at finances, so those tasks don't have to fall in his court.

Our limiting beliefs say there are tasks meant for men and tasks meant for women. These limit the potential of people everywhere to do what they love and offer it to the rest of us. And it keeps us stuck.

BELIEVING IT'S A PERMANENT CONDITION

When we're stuck, it's hard to see the current situation as temporary. This is especially true when our pain is deep. We're sad, mad, or overwhelmed and have convinced ourselves we'll always feel this way.

This is where the trouble starts. After we convince ourselves life is terrible because of this, that, or the other thing, we try to prove those beliefs to ourselves. We become our own worst enemy, sabotaging opportunities and friendships simply because our internal dialogue is so negative.

We often let our minds wander to past hurts. This causes us to make up a story about what will happen in the future based on what has happened in the past. It's a protective measure, to ensure that we are ready for the worst possible series of events and to avoid disappointment.

These stories rarely come true, but we suffer in the meantime.

What would you describe as a permanent problem?

IT'S NEVER TOO LATE TO CHANGE

Bob had a temper. He would let it out on his wife and children, but their friends and neighbors never knew. As his children grew and left the house, they had no desire to come back to the tongue lashing they were sure to get. Their time away became greater and greater, and Bob knew it.

Later in his life, Bob went through anger management training. He was motivated to reconnect with his children, and he called each one and asked to meet with them. It would have been easy for any of them to deny his request, believing his dysfunction was permanent. They could have written a story where their father, an angry and aggressive man, died alone *just like he deserved*. But they were willing to challenge those beliefs. They let him apologize for his bad behavior. Tears were shed, and reconciliation was cultivated. When Bob died, his children grieved the loss of their wonderful father.

Things can change in our lives. Holding onto the present and determining the future in our minds leaves us stuck.

We stay stuck when we feel our present circumstances are a permanent condition. But almost nothing is permanent. People and circumstances change.

Our present dire circumstances may just be telling us we're stuck. Stuck with conclusions. Stuck with fear. Stuck and overwhelmed. Stuck in so many ways. But if we see ourselves as *simply* stuck, we can open our minds to the possibility of change, improvement, and freedom.

Being stuck is never a permanent condition, unless we choose to make it so.

BELIEVING WE'RE NOT ENOUGH

Enough means as much as is required. Are you enough? Do you have what it takes to live a happy and successful life? Will you be able to weather the storms? Can you say with confidence you're satisfied with who you are?

We sometimes believe we're not enough. We look around and see what other people are accomplishing and wish we were achieving something great too. We see how others look and envy their beauty. Inevitably, there is always someone more accomplished, more beautiful, and happier than we are. We will always lose when we play the comparison game.

Don't play it. It will suck the life and potential right out of you. I know because I've done it.

In what ways do you feel you are not enough?

"Not enough" shows up in many ways. The most obvious is a person who berates themselves. A person who would not say an unkind word about anyone else feels completely comfortable doing it to themselves: *I'm not* (smart, rich, talented, resilient, focused, disciplined, brave, courageous, pretty, confident, patient) *enough to do that.* This kind of talk is self-focused and comes from the belief we are not enough. When we feel we aren't enough, we compare ourselves to others.

Healthy people don't think that way.

IF WE DON'T BELIEVE WE'RE ENOUGH, NEITHER WILL THEY

It went on for years. A circle of behaviors as crazy as a traffic circle with eight lanes. Sue would feel hurt and demand new behaviors from her husband. When Tom wouldn't do what she asked, she'd get angry and feel hurt again. Someone needed to step out of the circle.

She had a steady law practice, and Tom was an entrepreneur. He wanted to get involved in a new venture, which included borrowing more money than Sue was comfortable with. He needed her signature on the loan. She had a lot of questions about this new prospect, none of which Tom could answer completely.

It's been said that you teach people how to treat you. Sue taught her husband she'd stomp around and be mad but never follow through on her threats to change the dance. He could spend money Sue asked him not to spend. She'd be mad and pout and scream and cry. Then she'd scramble around and find the cash to make up for her husband's wasteful spending.

The real issue, however, had nothing to do with the business venture. The real issue was Sue wouldn't say no. She fretted and wrung her hands. She paced the floor and exploded with anger. She blamed him for asking but didn't have the courage to say no.

Sue didn't believe she was lovable and would do almost anything asked of her out of the fear of rejection.

The angst in her gut was like a ball of tangled string, as she feared denying his request meant he would leave her. The feeling that she wasn't enough was the problem.

Sue's belief she wasn't enough caused many problems in her life. The damage of this belief cost hundreds of thousands of dollars and almost cost her marriage. Saying yes when she meant no was bad for everyone. Doing something for someone else out of guilt, shame, or the lack of courage to say no doesn't work.

BELIEVING THE STORIES WE MAKE UP

Making up stories and believing them as truth is another way our beliefs limit our lives and get us stuck. When things don't go well, we feel compelled to figure out why. We want to be in the know. We're uncomfortable without all the information it takes to make sense of things, so we make up a story.

When we make up a story to fill in an uncomfortable gap, we convince ourselves the story is true and then seek to defend it. Our drive to have an answer trumps the truth.

There's an old and true saying—when you assume, you make an *ass* out of *u* and *me*.

You hear, "Joe doesn't eat dessert." Not understanding anyone not loving dessert, you come up with a story. "He must be some sort of health nut. Who doesn't eat dessert? He's probably so vain about his weight that he's become some sort of food Nazi." But the truth is, Joe is allergic to nuts. He doesn't have dessert because of the danger of an allergic reaction.

When we make up a story, we are often the main character. Other people's choices and preferences get squeezed into a play where we're the star. Instead of considering that each person is inside their own play, we take their words and actions when different from our own and come up with an explanation by making up a story.

Let's look at this example. Let's say your friend doesn't come to your party and you make up the story that she dislikes you. Because of your story, you avoid her. She picks up on that and distances herself from you too. Now you have proof that she doesn't like you because she's not calling as often. The story that she doesn't like you becomes ingrained. Then you hear she and her husband are having trouble and believe it's because she's so distant. More proof. The truth is, your friend was struggling with her husband's infidelity and couldn't bring herself to put on a happy face and come to your party. She was ashamed and afraid to tell anyone. Your story has damaged your relationship with her at a time she needs you the most.

We get stuck in a whirlwind of confusion when we believe the stories we've made up.

What story have you made up that may not be true?

BELIEVING THE JUDGMENTS OF OURSELVES

Another limiting belief is how we judge ourselves. We all make mistakes, some bigger than others. Those mistakes can last a lifetime in our minds, which keeps us stuck. The belief that what we've done is unforgivable or too big to ignore can cause us to be stuck.

HOLDING ON TO SELF-JUDGMENT

Pam was seventeen, rebellious, and working at a fast-food joint to earn her own money to buy the things her parents wouldn't. Her manager was married and in his twenties. He liked to flirt.

One thing turned into another, and soon they were having a full-blown affair. Eventually she broke it off, but the trauma of doing such an adult thing as a child stuck with her.

Pam stayed stuck in the judgment she held over herself that she was promiscuous. Then, at nineteen, she got pregnant by another man. Working to take care of her child, she never went to college. Pam felt she had disappointed her parents and was ashamed.

Believing she was damaged goods, Pam couldn't hear the recognition she received for her authentic spirit and smarts. Her judgment limited her and kept her from seeing she was relevant and useful in the business world. Pam worked hard but never believed she measured up to her coworkers. She spent most of her life believing she was unworthy because of the mistakes she had made in the past.

We judge the past and remember what we did then. Instead of seeing life as a progression of lessons, we get stuck reliving one, causing ourselves to stay ashamed and living in failure. The past is gone, and continuing to live in judgment keeps us stuck.

*What past judgments are you
holding that keep you stuck?*

SUMMARY

Our beliefs, left unchecked, lead us to being stuck. They can come from the different stereotypes we've believed about our gender or the limiting beliefs we've put on ourselves over time. We can be stuck believing the difficulties we're experiencing now are permanent instead of able to change for the better. A common problem is believing we're not enough, which keeps us unable to do the things we want to do. The beliefs we create when we make up stories also get us stuck in a world we made up. And finally, holding judgment over ourselves for past mistakes leads us to believe we're flawed permanently.

As we challenge our beliefs, we can get unstuck. What is the truth? Who are we when we believe those thoughts? Who would we be without them? What are we capable of if we confront these beliefs and form new ones?

Chapter Four

CONTROL

This chapter will discuss how we get stuck when we try to be in control. Our attempts to force things out of our control leave us frustrated. Other people resent us for trying to control their lives, judging their behavior, or holding them accountable. We pursue control and we get stuck.

When I was depressed, things seemed terribly out of control, so I sought to bring control to my life. I thought I was controlling my thoughts by obsessing over them. I couldn't control people, so I made up stories about who they were and what their motives were to soothe myself. I stubbornly held myself to unreal expectations, trying to control my world by making it perfect. My attempts to control came from a weak position and had me stuck.

We can try to control the past by holding onto resentment and regrets. Our attempts to control the present include striving for perfection, comparing ourselves to others, and being stubborn. The future feels like it can be controlled by setting unrealistic expectations.

All these methods make us stuck.

WE HOLD ON TO RESENTMENT

Stuff happens. Life is unfair. Sometimes we get the short end of the stick.

Yes, we've all had bad things happen to us, some worse than others. But holding on to resentment keeps us stuck.

Resentment is a nasty little emotion. Like a poisonous snake that hides under the bushes, it's ready to reach out and snatch your joy away at any moment. If you feed your resentment, it'll become bigger and even more vile.

Even more insidious than the original indignation, resentment will cause us to experience the betrayal over and over. As we recall an inequity, our memories snap into action and we relive the trauma all over again.

Resentment doesn't allow us to regain strength and confidence, and it breeds hatred, revenge, and envy. Hatred causes us stress. Revenge holds us captive as we plot the demise of our perpetrator. Envy makes us compare ourselves to others, which creates even more resentment.

Resentment can be hidden, and we may not even know we have it. It is, however, holding us stuck in a slurry of negative emotions that hold us captive in a place we want to move from.

What resentments are you holding that show you you're stuck?

WE HOLD ON TO REGRETS

We all have regrets. Some regret picking the wrong paint color for their bedroom, and others regret ending a relationship. Regretting the past is a problem of focus. The past is done, and focusing on our regrets causes nothing but pain. It leaves us stuck in limbo with no way to undo the reality of what happened.

Regrets can leave us stuck for years.

LOOKING FOR LOVE

Tom and Jill thought they were in love. Their sixteen-year-old selves had it all figured out. Kissing, passion, sex. It was natural.

So is pregnancy.

When Jill found out she was pregnant, Tom did an about-face and let her handle it on her own. They parted ways, the baby was born, and Tom was stuck with shame and regret. For the rest of his life, he defined himself by this event. He went into a shell and locked his emotions deep in the cellar. Unable to cope with his regret, he turned to alcohol, which didn't judge his behavior and gave him some relief. He was stuck.

Unable to discuss his regrets with anyone, Tom never forgave the hormone-driven boy he had been. He never considered Jill's part in the decision that changed both of their lives. He was stuck with regret, and it dictated the rest of his life.

Certainly, there are some mistakes with much bigger consequences than others. The result of Tom's actions had a name and was left without a father. This caused some serious emotional damage to all parties involved.

But when we continue to regret our past mistakes, we don't allow ourselves to move forward. We are stuck with the fantasy that we should have known better. We should have behaved better. We should have been better.

But we're all human. We didn't know better. We didn't behave better. We weren't better than we wished we had been. Holding onto regret ensures we will stay there. Holding onto regret is a way to continually punish ourselves.

Focusing on our regrets will keep us stuck.

What regret do you have that has you stuck?

PERFECTIONISM

Nothing's perfect. There is no perfect spouse, perfect job, perfect haircut, perfect phone, or perfect child. We know this, but we don't like to accept it. Perfectionism will always trip us up. Our attempts don't lead us closer to perfection; they crash and burn trying to meet a standard that cannot be met.

CAMPING

Six of us decided to go camping together. We were carefree twentysomethings with nothing but our careers, friends, and time and money to burn. Camping would be a blast! We'd probably be drinking beer around a campfire, laughing wildly at jokes, just like the commercials. Someone would bring a guitar. The fresh air and crumply leaves were calling my name.

I jumped right in and got busy planning. I decided when we would leave and who would bring what. It was two weeks away, and I was filled with anticipation. This would be *perfect!*

As we neared our departure, my friends began to waffle on the time we'd leave. Things were coming up. Although my perfect plans were unraveling, I refused to listen and kept pushing. This was going to be the perfect get-together with friends, food, laughter, and meaningful conversation.

When my roommate finally told me she didn't want to go, I exploded. "What? You committed to it! We are *all* going to go! We leave tomorrow!"

Instead of going with the flow, my thoughts were filled with malice toward these deadbeat friends who couldn't even follow through with what they said they were going to do. My perfect dream of a perfect vacation with perfect friends around a perfect campfire left me stuck. I had thrown my expectations on top of them. They either had to live up to them or lose my allegiance.

I was stuck.

My boyfriend gave me a new perspective. We talked about how things change. His carefree attitude allowed him to roll with it. His attitude stopped me dead in my tracks. He wasn't stuck holding his expectations over other people's lives. He easily accepted this change without judgment or frustration.

Somewhere in my unconscious, I knew I needed this attitude. So I married it.

What are you expecting to be perfect?

COMPARISONS

Almost everyone plays the comparison game. We look at someone and decide they're happier, richer, wiser, or have their whole life more together than us. This sets us up at a disadvantage. To cope, we either try to bring them down to our level (or lower) or boost ourselves up so we won't be the loser.

But it's always a losing proposition because there is always someone seemingly more accomplished, beautiful, or happy. Playing the comparison game gets us stuck. It causes us to focus on our insecurities and weakness.

Jealousy is a mean sister of comparison, and she's hard to get rid of. When we compare ourselves to the best, we'll always come up short. But if we compare ourselves to the worst, we'll always come out on top.

Which is it with you?

Who do you compare yourself to?

IT'S ALL RELATIVE

Bill was a good student. He performed well in high school, excelling in academics, athletics, and the arts. He got into a great college, and his future looked bright.

When he moved into the dorms freshman year, he immediately came face to face with the fact that he wasn't in Kansas anymore. His roommate had done well in high school too but had the distinction of getting a nearly perfect score on his ACT. Bill's classmates were at least as successful as he. It seemed that everywhere Bill went, he was faced with a person more successful than he.

One of his freshman classes was hard. Really hard. Bill struggled like he had never struggled before. In high school, assignments had been easy, and he got by without studying much at all. Now he spent hours upon hours studying and couldn't grasp the material well.

Bill asked some of his friends in the class if they understood what was going on. He got shrugs and "Sure, it's easy" or "Yeah, don't you?" He began to think something was wrong with him. He was failing the class. His self-esteem started to plummet, and he felt like one of the kids he had judged as dumb in high school who couldn't get good grades.

Comparing himself to those around him had Bill feeling defeated. He had used his academic intelligence to compare himself to others in order to feel superior. It was now crashing down on him, and the comparison game was his enemy.

Using comparison to help ourselves feel better is a way of controlling our discomfort. But we get stuck when we focus on others and compare ourselves to them. It's a bad habit and will eventually get us stuck.

How is the comparison game keeping you stuck?

STUBBORNNESS

Another way we try to control the present is stubbornness—showing dogged determination not to change our attitude or position on something, especially in spite of good arguments or reasons to do so.

There's some kind of mysterious line between determination and stubbornness. Determination moves us forward, while stubbornness digs in its heels and keeps us dead in our tracks. Determination tells us to ignore the naysayers, and stubbornness closes our ears to any new information at all. Determination is a willingness to live with the consequences of our decision, while stubbornness makes up a story that we're right no matter what.

When we're stubborn, we're rigid, like a board. Strength is good, but inflexibility ensures no movement will take place. When push comes to shove, a stiff board will snap in two. But when we're determined, the goal is bigger than our ego. We listen to new input and allow it to change our direction if useful. This flexibility moves us forward to our goal.

Sometimes people call us out on our stubbornness. As stubborn people, certain we are right, we will not let new information get by the gates. Our behavior will stay the same. It takes humility to let go of stubbornness and allow others to help. Accepting new information will get us unstuck.

Stubborn people resist help from others, but if we truly want to get unstuck, we will seek out counsel from others. Putting aside our pride, we will ask what needs to be done to fix the problem keeping us stuck.

What stubborn ideas are keeping you stuck in unhealthy ways of living?

UNREALISTIC EXPECTATIONS

We can get frustrated when the circumstances, the economy, or our partners don't live up to our expectations. Our frustration, however, is just a sign that our expectations aren't matching reality and we are waiting for them to line up—but, in truth, we are stuck.

Unrealistic expectations from a parent can cause an impressionable child to get stuck, frozen in the demands and not wanting to disappoint them. These unrealistic expectations cause harm.

Many people get stuck with unrealistic expectations of others because they expect a lot from themselves. If I want my house neat and tidy, I infer everyone else does too. When my spouse or children leave a mess, I get mad because they don't hold the same value of cleanliness that I have. My unrealistic expectations cause frustration.

I'm stuck.

GIFTS

For years I asked my husband for a specific gift for Christmas. For three years, he bought me something else. I never understood how he could be so dense and was frustrated he wouldn't meet my expectations. After the third year of asking for a Pilates video but getting something else, it dawned on me how silly I'd been. I'd been stuck expecting him to take step A—buying me that video—before I'd go on to step B: trying Pilates at home.

What I discovered is that he likes to give surprises! Buying me what I asked for seemed ridiculous to him. I have been stuck many times in my life because of my own unrealistic expectations.

Expectations start in childhood. We learn to expect that Dad will make dinner or Mom will be asleep at nine o'clock.

Whatever behaviors happen in our home, we see them as normal and expect these actions.

As we grow in adulthood, we meet people with different expectations of what is normal and right. This can cause us frustration if we bring those into marriage. Sometimes, we insist our way of thinking is right.

It's okay to come up with our own expectations for spirituality, cleanliness, friendships, health, and life, but it is unrealistic to require others to follow suit. It's only when we allow others to be different that can we be free of unrealistic expectations.

We also get stuck when we try to fit into the expectations others have of us. When we do something just to be accepted, we build up frustration. It's not the other person's expectation causing us to be stuck but our lack of courage to say what we will and won't do. It's unwise to follow another person's unrealistic expectations.

What unrealistic expectations do you
have for yourself or others?

SUMMARY

Our desire to control our life can get us stuck. We relive resentments of the past in an effort to control the memory. We do the same with regrets, and they don't serve us well. As we strive toward perfectionism and play the comparison game, we don't control our lives as much as try to force them into a predetermined mold. And our stubbornness and unrealistic expectations show our desire to control things we feel uncomfortable with.

Each of these pursuits gets us stuck. Identifying where you fall into these traps is a great place to start moving your life from the place it is stuck.

Chapter Five

SKILLS

WE DON'T KNOW WHAT TO DO

Another reason we stay stuck is that, even though we know we're stuck, we just don't know what to do next.

We can be stuck not knowing how to proceed with a relationship because we don't know what conversation to have, how to explain ourselves better, or what boundaries to set. We can be stuck without hope because we don't know how to see the glass as half-full or the benefits of being grateful. We can be stuck overweight, not knowing how to eat right and exercise properly.

When I was depressed, I truly did not know what to do. The "experts" couldn't help me. This left me alone, pre-Google, wondering what my next step should be. No one wanted to talk about depression, and most people didn't understand. So books became my ally. This lonely pursuit taught me to keep my eyes, ears, and heart open for every opportunity, no matter how crazy it seemed. Every time I learned something new, I put it into practice, hoping to rid myself once and for all of this terrible disease.

We can wander through our days with a gut feeling there is more to life, but we don't know how to find out what that is. Do I go to church? Do I read a book? Do I follow popular culture?

Do I pray, meditate, or lie in the sun? Do I get back to nature, go on a silent retreat, or walk the Camino de Santiago?

Imagine you're stuck with a child going down the wrong path. She drinks alcohol as a minor, and you suspect she's doing drugs too. What do you do? Order a drug test? Talk to her about it? Trust her even though she's lied to you repeatedly? Believe the best in her? Nothing? Send her to treatment? Ship her off to your sister's house because she'll be able to deal with her? Pray? Ask friends?

Not knowing what to do next keeps us stuck.

If time or money were no object, how could you solve your problem?

Figuring out what to do requires a lot of trial and error. Not everything we try is helpful to get us unstuck. We must be open to all the possibilities. Listen to others, do your own research, be self-reflective, and ask good friends. Remember, you do not need to stay stuck. There is always a solution, and you are the one who will benefit the most by finding it.

In my experience, it was my responsibility to find out what skills I needed. The first skill seemed to fall in my lap. After that, I kept my eyes and ears open to any possible solution to free me from depression. Slowly I discovered the skills to set me free.

WE DON'T HAVE THE SKILLS TO GET UNSTUCK

Having an open mindset and the humility to change is imperative to getting unstuck. There is always a way to improve our circumstances, but that way may include learning a new skill. There is no age at which we've learned all we can.

Without the necessary skills, we stay stuck. If we don't know the skill of eating right, we'll probably be stuck overweight. If we don't have the mental health skills to negotiate, we'll be stuck not getting what we want. If we don't learn any spiritual health skills, we'll be stuck unfulfilled.

When I was depressed, I didn't have the skills to cope well with life. I was unskilled in a combination of physical, mental, and spiritual ways. These unskilled, undisciplined, or immature ways led to sad and depressed thoughts, which made me difficult to get along with and despondent about my life. I was stuck because I didn't have the skills.

These skills don't necessarily come along naturally. Just because you're eighteen years old and classified as an adult does not mean you know how to take care of your body. Just because you are married and have children doesn't mean you have the mental health skills to be a good parent. And just because you're retired and have had a successful career does not mean you have a well-rounded understanding of life.

How do you get the skills to get unstuck? You're going to have to learn them! This is important for everyone to know. Without the effort to learn a new skill, we will stay stuck. These skills may be difficult at first, but learning them will be easier than staying stuck.

What new skills will you try to get unstuck?

It's also important to believe a new skill will actually help get you unstuck. At one point, I was told my body was reacting to all the chemicals in my life, so for two years, I didn't wear any makeup. For me, that was a big deal! My emotional pain, however, was greater than my vanity (which was pretty big in those days), and I agreed to give it a try.

Another recommendation I got was to stop taking the antidepressant I was on. That was a scary proposition, but with a doctor's help, I went off and have not taken any since. My depression went away with methods other than medication.

My journey through depression had me stuck. It wasn't until the obvious methods failed that I was forced to figure out how to heal myself. It was clear things weren't working in my life, so I needed new physical, mental, and spiritual health skills.

The combination of new skills I learned got me unstuck from depression. They also helped me to become healthier than I have been my entire life.

WE'RE FOCUSED ON WHAT WE DON'T HAVE

Recently I discovered, after a lifetime of seeing things in two dimensions (instead of three like almost everyone else), I could train my eyes and brain to work together to see three dimensions. This will be the source of another book, I'm sure. After one dramatic breakthrough, I drove down streets saying out loud, "I can't believe this is what everyone else sees!" Little children and old men see the world with dimension and perspective I had been incapable of perceiving.

My focus had been off—*literally*. Interestingly and mercifully, I didn't know what I was missing. It's the same with each one of us. When our focus is off, we don't have a complete perspective. When we focus simply on what we don't have, we don't see a complete picture. Our vision is skewed.

When we see the glass as half empty, we focus on what we don't have instead of what we do. If your focus is on scarcity, it's a sure sign you're stuck.

When I was depressed, I would think about how sad everything seemed, how awful people were to me, how bad my life was. The habit of focusing on what I didn't have made me stuck.

To help you see whether you are focusing on the wrong thing, see if you find yourself in any of these statements.

My spouse is not around to help.

I'm sick of staying home with these kids.

I don't have any friends.

I'm so tired.

I wish I had the money the Joneses had!

I'm so fat.

My family hates me.

My job is the worst.

Now let's switch it around and start with, "What I *do* have is . . ." and then say something positive. If this doesn't come easily to you, be aware of how your thoughts are pointing to the negative instead of positive. You simply have the wrong focus.

What I do have is a spouse who works very hard.

What I do have are healthy kids. They laugh and play along without crying and fighting. I am grateful they are healthy, and I'm not spending my days caring for chronic health needs.

What I do have is the opportunity to make friends. I just need to figure out how to get over my fear of reaching out to others. I have a good mind and opportunities all around me.

What I do have is an opportunity to figure out why I just can't make it through the days without feeling sluggish. Is it my diet? Am I getting enough sleep? Am I managing my stress? Do I have support?

What I do have is enough money for what I need now. What the Joneses have has nothing to do with me. Comparison is a buzzkill.

What I do have is a body. Think about what it can do. It's amazing to be able to read and laugh. I can clean the house and dance if I want.

What I do have is a family. I can't absolutely know how they feel about me, but they are all entitled to their opinion. I will love the family I have.

What I do have is a job. Whether or not it's good is up to me. If it's not meeting my needs, I can change it.

What are you focusing on that you don't have?

Each of us can use our minds to focus on a broader view of all that is around us and see in more than one or two dimensions. When we're focused on what we *don't* have, we'll be stuck.

TAKING THE BAIT

We may be stuck because we're taking the bait from a sick, sad, or skeptical person. They are stuck and want us to join them in their mud puddle. They sit with their fishing rod and throw bait out in front of us. It can be juicy gossip or anger toward a common enemy. The bait can be shame or envy. This bait can draw us in like a fish to a minnow and cause us to get stuck.

OUR SON SOLD A CAR

Our son tried to sell his car on Craigslist. I was happy to hear he had priced it so low that a bidding war was going on. A few days later, my husband got a very long text from an anonymous sender.

It became clear after a few sentences that the author was very unhappy the listed price had gone up. Apparently, he had gone to quite a bit of trouble to find out who his foe's father was. We don't live in the same city but are connected in business. He then detailed his unhappiness in what turned out to be several paragraphs. The last sentence was, "I'd be very ashamed of my child if he did what your son did."

I took the bait.

I went into my investigator mode and wanted all the details so I could determine who was right and who was wrong. I was sinking into the mud. I tried to reason it out. What was the purpose of the text? Did he want us to bring our son home and spank him for being such a bad person? He was thirty!

My husband's more logical reaction was to tell the texter, "Thank you, I'll pass this on to my son." He didn't take the bait from this anonymous texter. As it turned out, Mr. Texter had never come to look at the car, test-driven it, or made an offer, but his disappointment that others wanted to pay more for the car than he did sent him into a texting rage.

We get stuck when we join those who are stuck in their mud puddle. I was ready to jump right in with Mr. Texter and argue about a situation that had absolutely nothing to do with me.

We get stuck when we take the bait.

THE BAIT OF GOSSIP

It's tough to stop gossip once it's made its way into a conversation. Recently, a friend said, "I had this terrible experience! This woman was *so* mean to me! She did [blah blah blah] and it made me feel awful!" She then continued in hushed tones, "Do you want to know who it was?"

No, I really don't . . . but I kinda do.

As I argued with myself about how to answer her question, I left enough of a pause that my friend spilled the beans and gave me a name. Dang it. Now I was judging the gossipee based on a conversation I wasn't a part of and of whose story I only got one side. That judgment would stick to my shoes and feel tacky the next time I saw the object of my friend's discontent.

It's messy business.

Gossip is like having gum stuck in your hair. It's hard to get rid of. Once we hear it, it's hard to get out of our minds. But just like gum removal, it can be done. Beware of the sticking potential of gossip, and run from it if you can.

What bait have you taken that has you stuck?

COMMON ENEMY

I knew a woman who was difficult for me to deal with. She pushed my boundaries and asked for things I wasn't comfortable with. I looked for reasons to explain my disdain for her. Any small error on her part caused me to spew with anger and spread nasty words about her.

I looked for others who had dealt with this woman to see if we could blather about her questionable ethics. It felt so good to have someone on my side, as if that made her *more* wrong. Pulling my coconspirator into the mud with me felt good, for the moment.

But creating this common enemy caused me to be even more stuck. There were now two of us in the mud. To forgive and move on meant each of us had to admit our failure and come to a new conclusion. That was complicated because we each had our own perspective. It very possibly fueled his distaste for this woman and got him even more stuck than before.

Creating common enemies is easy. It's child's play. It's chicken.

It's a good way to get stuck.

SUMMARY

Our lack of skills is a way we get stuck. They point out lessons we need to learn to have a better life. Sometimes we just don't know what to do. When I struggled with depression and heard of something that might help, I often needed new skills. I had to stop focusing on what I didn't have and being so reactive to those around me. It was only through growth that I was able to beat it.

Chapter Six
BAD THINGS WE DO WHILE WE'RE STUCK

WE COMPLAIN

Complaining gives a voice to our unhappiness. This feeds negative intentions and emotions. As tangible as a hammer hitting a nail, those words have power. They fan the flames of discontent in our heart. They agitate those around us, asking them to join our misery. Those complaints are a sure sign we are stuck.

It's easy to complain. Social media has given us a platform to complain to a large group of people with a few strokes of the keyboard. We hide behind our screens, lashing out at what's wrong with the world, assuring our lives remain in the same unhappy state.

We're stuck.

What is one thing you complain about?

It starts innocently enough. In Minnesota, we complain about the weather, mosquitoes, and road construction. We add a complaint to whatever good thing has happened as if to bring it back down to earth and keep ourselves humble. We complain about our favorite sports team letting us down and fancy ourselves experts as we explain how we'd do things differently.

Our complaints are met with nods of agreement or sad eyes complicit in the exchange. Grumbling is a national pastime. It's the opposite of seeing the world with rose-colored glasses.

Complaining is a sure sign we have the wrong focus and are stuck.

WE HYPERBOLIZE

Teenagers hyperbolize. In their defense, they have very little perspective, so when they don't have a date for the senior prom, life can seem to be at its end. Most of their peers are also operating with hormones in overdrive and not much ability to take control of their circumstances. Exaggerating their plight is a coping mechanism that's both tolerated and accepted in our culture.

Adults can also hyperbolize. A demanding boss can cause us to feel like we don't have much ability to control our circumstances. We tell our friends, calling our boss controlling and cold. Often, we'll find others to join our "I Hate the Boss" club. We exaggerate the boss's behavior and talk about how the company is suffering under such an incompetent manager.

We get stuck.

Hyperbole isn't a skill we want to develop, and using it won't help us get unstuck. Listening to it won't either. Exaggeration simply exacerbates the problem. It takes more energy to exaggerate the problem than solve it.

What words are you using to exaggerate a situation?

We Get Pessimistic

Because of our twenty-four-hour appetite for breaking news, we often find out about horrible events. We've witnessed a parade of womanizers, insane criminals, weather anomalies, extreme politicians, pedophiles, and school shooters. These crazy, bizarre stories have become commonplace because we're regularly exposed to them. Advertisers drool as their products show up on specials that lay out the gory details of the most recent hideous act.

And we've become pessimistic. There is no doubt these tragedies are awful and take a cruel toll on humankind. We take in an excessive number of details of these events. Do we really need to know how the little children were gunned down and the timeline? I'm not voting for putting our heads in the sand, but the details of these rare events are noxious, and feeding the curious but twisted part of us will lead us straight to a dead end.

The amount of sad news we take in each day can lead us into thinking our lives are filled with potential perils. The bizarre becomes commonplace and our pessimism grows. We are no longer shocked by rare events because we're fed a healthy diet of the extraordinary. Soon, we expect terrible things to come our way and lose hope in the good of mankind.

The excess coverage and details are causing personal damage and making us stuck. We're becoming fearful, anxiety worn, and cynical about each event's outcome. I overheard some people glued to the TV over a "crazed man" who had escaped from a mental institution on the other side of the country. They were obviously worried this lunatic might disrupt their day and needed to keep on the lookout.

These people became stuck because the TV had alerted them to a distant threat, which became very real in their minds. Their distrust of humankind led them to be concerned with their own fears even though the perpetrator was last seen a thousand miles away.

We've become pessimistic and lost our perspective. Almost all of us live ordinary lives. We get up to an alarm, eat breakfast, go about our day, come home, make supper, and find something to entertain us before we go to bed. We eat, we sleep, we enjoy those around us. That's it. That's enough! That's life.

Most of us don't have neighbors who are serial killers or shop at malls where bombs go off. Most of us won't be the victim of a drive-by shooting. The news of these events, however, has caused us to lose faith in other people's motives. We see a boogeyman around every corner, and it's making us stuck.

We're not open to new opportunities because of our growing pessimism. It can also lead us to make poor choices as we feed on the bad news du jour. These poor choices leave us stuck, and we're not free.

What are you pessimistic about?

IGNORING OUR PROBLEMS

Ignoring our problems doesn't make them go away; it starts a snowball effect. One problem sticks to another, creating an even bigger problem. Suddenly, the problem becomes so big it seems impossible to face. Childhood problems not dealt with become issues in marriage. Not caring for our body turns into chronic aches and pains. Cynicism turns into anger or hopelessness.

When we turn away from our problems, we start a process where small problems can cause life-changing damage. By ignoring the problem, things become worse, not better.

TOO BUSY TO LISTEN

John and Sally were a beautiful couple. They had lots of friends and a full life. They were so busy running here and there that they didn't take time to sit down face to face to let each other know what their deepest needs were. It was only in hurried frustration that Sally let John know she wasn't happy with how things were going. John ignored her plea. He believed continuing to make a large salary would keep her secure. She didn't insist that things needed fixing.

They had four beautiful children. Not stopping to enjoy this new phase in their life, they piled on more obligations and parties. Always on the go, no one would have guessed that their relationship was hanging by a thread, least of all John. Sally's tired appeals to slow things down were met with misunderstanding.

Until Sally had an affair.

John and Sally's life had been what our culture admired. Deep beneath it all, however, their relationship wasn't being cared for. It needed them to listen to each other and have long conversations. It needed a respite from all John's "fun" activities, technology overload, and the desire to control his climb to the top. It needed Sally to assert the emptiness she felt.

She found what she desperately needed in the listening ear of another. It was like a drug. She allowed her emotions to determine her next step. This new man filled the emptiness she felt with John. When John found out, he was completely shocked.

No one meant for this to happen, and the results were traumatic. They had been stuck not listening, stuck not standing firm with feelings of discontent, stuck in busyness, stuck focusing on what they didn't yet have, and stuck letting emotions dictate behavior. They could have been permanently stuck, but they faced their inadequacies and got through it.

*What small problems are you not addressing
that could create a snowball effect?*

SUMMARY

There are all kinds of bad habits we develop while we're stuck. I was a master at complaining about all that was wrong with the world when I was depressed. I exaggerated things in my mind and became cynical about the possibility of things ever changing for the better. This kept me stuck.

Although it's uncomfortable to take responsibility for our bad behaviors, it's necessary to living our best life.

Living a healthy life is going to be a no-brainer once we see the damage done when we don't. This isn't rocket science. You each know this but can be sidetracked by quick fixes. The truth is, living a stuck life, unable to do what you want, is *way* harder than the work it takes to improve things. This simple principle along with a few tips on how to get healthy physically, mentally, and spiritually will jettison the bad habits out of your life for good.

Chapter Seven

THE FINAL REASON WE'RE STUCK

WE WON'T TAKE A STEP

Getting healthy—physically, mentally, and spiritually—is the answer. Once we put aside our fears and uncomfortable feelings and believe our strength can save us, we will live healthy, happy, and content lives. Our weaknesses will be in the past, we will proceed with the steps necessary in small increments, and satisfaction will replace our disappointments.

As we move toward a healthy life, our focus will become clear. We'll figure out the precise steps to take and rid ourselves of the coping mechanisms not serving us well. We will realize how each element of our new health builds on the previous one. The power of all three is the secret. It's not complicated or difficult.

But before we move to this beautiful place, we need to confront one more piece of the puzzle. This is the basis for why we are where we are. We are stuck simply because we won't take a step. We may be waiting for someone else to fix our problems. Or we lack the courage, energy, or self-love it will take.

What small step could you take to get unstuck?

WE'RE WAITING FOR SOMEONE ELSE TO RESCUE US

Just like Sleeping Beauty, who slept until Prince Charming awakened her, many of us live like we are damsels in distress. We wait for someone else to take us out of our misery and improve our lives.

Except it's *our* life.

This doesn't necessarily have anything to do with gender. It can take many forms:

When my boss stops being so bossy, I'll be happy.

When my spouse changes, it will take care of my negative emotions, our finances, and my weaknesses.

When the weather gets better, I'll be in a better mood.

When my children grow up, I'll be happy with them.

My ailments will be cured when my doctor prescribes the right pill.

I'll be hopeful when my life is perfect.

I'll get together with my friends when they call me.

That thing will get taken care of when someone else takes care of it.

---

*Who are you expecting will swoop in
and take care of your problems?*

In my journey with depression, I waited for many years not knowing what was wrong. When I received a diagnosis, I believed a little white pill would solve my troubles. When medications failed, I looked to counselors to explain my sadness. There was nothing to uncover. Finally, I asked God to rescue me. He was silent.

The truth was the next step was mine. I lost precious years waiting for someone else to step in and rescue me. I was the only one who could take the wheel and right the ship. It was up to me.

WE DON'T HAVE THE COURAGE TO STEP FORWARD

The definition of courage is *the ability to do something that frightens one*, or *strength in the face of pain or grief*.

When we don't have the courage to do something that needs to be done, we are stuck.

THE ABILITY TO DO SOMETHING THAT FRIGHTENS ME

In 1991, thanks to my husband's awesome skills at work with his generous employer, we were given money to go on a trip anywhere in the world. Our boys were one and four at the time, so it didn't make sense to bring them. The idea of flying over the ocean was a very scary proposition to me. Fear started the "what if" questions. What if we died? What if the boys got sick while we were away? What if I don't understand the language and they don't understand English? What if we get ripped off? What if there is some sort of emergency at home and we can't get back? What if I can't drink the water? What if our boys are sad we're gone? What if, what if, what if . . . ?

I tried to short-circuit the gift because I didn't have the courage. As I fretted and fussed about the decision, I asked my mom what she would do. "The boys seem too young to leave for ten days," I reasoned.

My mom looked at me and said, "Oh, kids! They won't even

know you're gone." I took her advice, swallowed deeply, and got the courage to say yes.

My mom's words helped me get unstuck. Because of that, we went on the trip of a lifetime. It expanded our perspective of history, architecture, and rest. When each of our boys reached seventeen, we did it again, understanding the money spent was well worth the experience.

Our lack of courage is one of the basic reasons we're stuck. Behind that lack of courage can lie fear.

STRENGTH IN THE FACE OF PAIN OR GRIEF

It's my life's purpose to get up in front of people and talk about my battle with depression. I find meaning and purpose as I explain the journey to others who may themselves be depressed or know someone who is. Maybe my struggle can help them understand what is going on and how to find a way out.

Almost every time I give a presentation, someone will come up to me and tell me how courageous I am. It's always a curious comment to me. Courage? I don't feel that way. I'm just telling my story. There is no more shame in my mind for having depression than there is for having breast cancer or a broken leg.

I suppose sharing my story can be defined as courageous. But it's way easier than the journey itself. Fighting the disease required and developed courage.

Now that I've beaten depression, I can do anything!

It was hard to cry that intensely. It's hard to be that angry, spitting and screaming my discontent with everything in my life. It's hard to be exhausted by a body that's weak. It's impossible to muster up any hope in a life that feels pointless and sad. The days were long, and the nights were even longer.

The courage came when I was facing pain and grief. This may be a testament to how difficult depression can be. Standing in front of others explaining the dirty details, which may seem like glaring weaknesses, pales in comparison to the journey itself.

What is it you haven't had the courage to do?

Here are some of the things I found to develop courage.

Desperation: When we're desperate enough, we do what it takes. We do it when we're in love, when we're in danger, or when we desire something enough. When we get desperate, we find the courage needed.

Accomplishment: As we go through life and succeed at this or that, our confidence grows. It feels good! Our newfound confidence gives us courage to try new things, hoping for even more success. Confidence is a close cousin to courage.

Encouragement: Other people's encouragement can give us courage. If we trust their words and motivations, we can become courageous beyond what we're able to muster up ourselves. My mom's encouragement to fly overseas and be away from our children gave me the courage I needed.

Beliefs: Our beliefs can spur on and increase our courage. If I believe in my abilities, I will develop the courage to try new things. If I believe in my company's desire to promote from within, I'll be courageous enough to apply for a new position. If I believe in a divine creator who will protect me, I'll be courageous in the face of potential threats.

Love: Love also develops courage. We can love others courageously, not considering the impact on us. We can have strength in the face of pain or grief. Love strengthens our courage.

Our lack of courage to face the pain and grief keeps us stuck. You must believe me when I tell you this principle. There is freedom on the other side of it. The battle may seem difficult, but being stuck in it is more difficult yet. To get unstuck, you have to muster up enough courage to face your pain and grief.

WE WON'T ENGAGE IN SELF-CARE

Self-care does not mean you have manicures weekly, sleep fourteen hours a day, and only do what you want to do. Self-care is living your life in the healthiest way possible. It means you consider what you eat the fuel for your life. It means you protect yourself from people who drain you emotionally. It means you invest time in prayer or meditation.

A lack of self-care is probably the biggest reason many of us stay stuck. We don't take care of our body, mind, or spirit. Maybe we're getting something out of not being cared for. Sympathy? Attention? Acceptance from others who are stuck?

Or is it just a bad habit?

What self-care are you lacking?

Self-care is like car maintenance. We need to put gas in the tank and change the oil so that we aren't left by the side of the road. When we hear a weird noise, we have to take it to the shop or investigate what the problem is. The problem must be fixed. If not, we are left with a vehicle that can't get us from point A to point B.

Self-care is the same. It's necessary to take care of our body, mind, and spirit to have a good life. Routine maintenance is necessary to keep us going.

Without doing these things, our lives don't work. They figuratively have flat tires and overheated engines. We cannot be productive and happy if we aren't caring for the basic elements of our life that make them go. Self-care is stopping to ask yourself what you need and making sure you take care of it.

It all starts with us. All the things that get us stuck are merely a reflection of what we need to change. They are actually gifts to us. The mud is a sign.

The lotus grows in the mud. It is undeterred by its dirty environment and miraculously blooms each day. It defies logic. You are the same. The mud around you is serving to grow you. But much more than a flower, you are able to make choices and see possibilities.

You can bloom every day too.

WE WON'T GROW UP

Our parents did the best they could. Unfortunately, many of us didn't get what we needed as children because our parents didn't have the skills to give it. This can cause a lifetime of pain. We got stuck because we weren't loved, nurtured, or cared for properly. We grow into adults and carry the pain with us.

It's reasonable to feel the pain when you're a child, but as you become an adult, these emotional pains become your responsibility. The pain can be a sticking point if it isn't dealt with. Seeing your parents as flawed human beings, just like you are, is a big step toward getting unstuck.

I was well into my forties before I realized the expectations I put on my parents were unrealistic. I expected them to call every week, support and encourage me in every one of my endeavors, and be 100 percent interested in my life, regardless of how little I cared about theirs.

Parents will always have a special place in our lives. But they're just people. They are simply adults we have a relationship with. They are not superhuman, like we pictured as children.

They do not know everything, as we may have believed earlier in our lives. We get stuck when we don't grow up from our childish thinking.

Our parents have their own struggles, personalities, and flaws. Their bodies are older than ours and need more care. They've lived more life and have a different perspective than us. When we learn to accept who our parents are, aside from what we imagined as children, we will be less likely to get stuck.

When we have unresolved feelings from our childhood, we often don't know what to do with them. As long as we continue thinking of ourselves as children and acting as we did as children, we won't be able to move forward in our lives. These unresolved feelings turn into distorted beliefs about how things should be. They have far-reaching effects in all our relationships.

How are you still acting like a child in your relationship with your parents?

How are you still acting like a parent in your relationship with your adult children?

It's difficult to move from a childish relationship with our parents to an adult one. And even if we decide to change, they may not. As we all know, the only person we can change is ourselves. Without growing into an adult in the relationship, we are bound to be stuck, allowing and believing things must remain as they did when we were young.

To get unstuck, we need to start acting like an adult.

WE WON'T GO TO THE EFFORT OF CHANGING THINGS

Children can find it hard to clean their room because it's too big. It seems like it will take a year to put all their toys away. Even though the consequences may mean no TV time, they won't clean because it looks like it will take too much effort.

As adults, we can be stuck because it seems too darn hard to make things better. Even if we believe things can be better, the effort may seem too daunting. We won't make an effort.

When we won't take a step to change, we're stuck. We're stuck with how things are right now. Step back and look at your life from a distance. Are you the person who wants things to be different but won't expend the effort to get there?

JUST TAKE CARE OF IT

We got Sophie because our sons wanted a dog. Pets are good for kids. It's something for them to snuggle and kiss when they get to those awkward teenage years and will no longer show affection to their parents.

We bought an electric fence to keep her safely in our backyard. To save money, we purchased it at the local hardware store and decided to install it ourselves. It got partially buried and partially laid on the ground.

We didn't follow the rest of the instructions to train Sophie to use the fence. A squirrel chewed a part of it, and it went unfixed for months. The battery in the collar went bad, and we neglected to change it.

My embarrassment grew as we routinely got messages on our answering machine like, "Um . . . do you have a dog named Sophie? She's at our house." One neighbor actually confessed to me she had the kids hide when Sophie came over because she knew the dog would want to come in if she heard children's voices.

Sophie regularly ran across the electric fence line, through the park, and over to the house with kids and snacks. At one point she scratched a hole in a screen door, which we apologetically repaired.

Because we didn't go to the effort of changing things, Sophie learned there wasn't a fence in our yard at all. We were stuck with a disobedient dog because we hadn't done things right in the first place.

Taking care of the things we needed to do to keep our dog from wandering would have been easier on us—and our neighbors.

---

*What have you not been willing
to do that has you stuck?*

SUMMARY

Although our fears, feelings, beliefs, desire for control, and lack of skills get us stuck, our unwillingness to make a change is what keeps us there. No one else can do it but you. It will take courage and self-care. It requires growing up and exerting the effort. There is no other way out.

The shortest path between two points is a straight line, but that only happens when things line up perfectly. There is a reason you're stuck, and the journey out will not be linear. Hopefully just knowing this will alleviate some frustration when things don't go smoothly.

It's hard work to stay in unhealthy patterns. Living in an unhealthy body and having an unhealthy mind or spirit takes more effort than what it will take to free yourself. The steps may not seem worth it, but that's not true. Each part of the journey will get easier. As you shed the difficult, unhealthy habits from your life, you will rise from the puddle and find a new freedom you may never have thought possible.

Section Two

WHY GET UNSTUCK?

We know we're stuck. But the thought of change is daunting. We understand things aren't working the best for us. But at least they're familiar. We're comfortable with the familiar. But we envy those doing things differently. We want to look better. We want to feel better. We want to do better.

So now what?

Do you know what being stuck is keeping you from? What would you like to have? How would you like to feel? When do you want it to happen?

What is being stuck in an unhealthy body keeping you from? Energy to do the things you want? Good sleep? Clothes you feel good in? A positive self-image? A positive attitude? Flexibility? Strength? A strong immune system? Clear thinking?

You might say, "But I want comfort!"

At what cost?

What is being stuck with emotional baggage keeping you from? Happiness? Opportunity? Healthy relationships? Confidence? Solutions? Laughter? Freedom? Ownership?

You might say, "But I don't want to change!"

At what cost?

What is your skepticism keeping you from? Love? Joy? Hope? Understanding? Peace? Certainty? Gratefulness? Meaning?

You might say, "But I don't want to look like a fool!"

At what cost?

My Story

It took thirty-five years. Tears, pain, drama, exhaustion, hopelessness, and planning my demise. The sad, tangled ball of pain had desperation at its core. The desperation threatened to take me out and was only overpowered by my desperation to survive. The survival instinct kept me searching for answers. It kept looking for a way to alleviate the misery.

THE BEACH

Growing up, Shady Oak Beach was a magical place for my family. We often went to splash around in the water and make castles in the sand. It was free entertainment for our family of seven. There is one black-and-white picture of me from that time. I stood wearing what I remember as a lime-green one-piece with fabric flower pedals attached. The pedals drooped, but I loved that bathing suit. I stood there with my belly protruding toward the camera. My right eye is closed as I squinted toward the sun, the sand pail by my side. I was about six years old.

When I was young, I had a terrible experience at the beach. Trying out the new skills I had learned in swimming lessons, I confidently went out to the dock I could stand next to and decided to float on my back to the other dock in equally shallow water. I gazed up at the sky, floating on my back and using my arms to move.

My peaceful swim was interrupted as I bumped into a group of teenagers throwing a ball to one other. I went to stand up, but my feet didn't touch the ground. I went under and swallowed a mouthful of lake water. I panicked and choked. The teenagers didn't see me. I struggled to get to the surface only to drop down into the water again. I was drowning.

Coughing, choking, and no ability to scream for help. Panic and fear. Images from my past. I remember seeing the surface, but there was no way to get there. Like being trapped at the bottom of a hole with no ladder to climb out and no air to breathe. This was the end. I wanted my mom and dad. I wanted to get out. I didn't want to die.

One of the teenagers must have noticed what was going on and grabbed me from below the surface. I clung to him as tight as I could as I coughed and spewed the green lake water out of my lungs. He carried me to the shore, where I didn't want to let go of the stranger who had been my rescue.

I would have done anything to get above the surface. *Anything.* That's what it's like to be desperate.

When depression took me below the surface, I kept fighting and grasping. The only other option was to give up and die. But I was desperate and wanted to live. The surface I could see was the lives of people who didn't live underneath sadness and hopelessness. There had to be a way out. There had to be a way to breathe.

Desperation leads to change. When I was depressed, I was stuck being unhappy. I had bad relationships. I constantly felt sluggish. I was not content. I had no confidence. I felt no hope about the future. I was disappointed with my abilities. I was stuck in fear, anxiety, tiredness, worthlessness, despair, and hopelessness. I could not see how things could get better. My constant underlying feeling was anguish.

It didn't have to be that way for me, and it doesn't have to be that way for you. Figuring out what stuck is keeping us from will be inspiration to change.

Some need to hit rock bottom. Others need to feel they're at the end of their rope. And still others need to simply decide they are fed up with the pain.

What is being stuck keeping you from?

Chapter Eight

WHAT WILL IT TAKE?

It's a Worthy Effort

Getting unstuck takes time.

There's no doubt about it.

It takes change. Our old ways will need to be discarded for good.

It has to be done.

Being stuck takes effort too. It's difficult, burdensome, and tiring. It has you exhausted, frustrated, and blue. Make no mistake, it's hard work to stay in the mud puddle, splashing around in the dysfunction that put you there. Wouldn't you like to get out?

To gain freedom, a revolution has to happen. It doesn't have to be dramatic and treacherous. Just change. Something new. Small steps. One little adjustment in how you go about your day. Followed by another. The steps will be tough. But it's tougher not to take them.

Some of those steps will be difficult or awkward. You may stumble along the way or wander off in the wrong direction and find out something doesn't work. It's like a GPS rerouting when we take a wrong turn. It happens to everyone. No one can give you the perfect directions. You will figure them out as you go.

But just keep moving. It will be easier than repeating the same steps you are taking today, which have you walking in a circle around your difficulty. It's hard work to be disappointed with your spouse every single day. It's troublesome to live without purpose. It's burdensome to live in a body that is tired, achy, and inflexible.

What hard work are you enduring by staying stuck?

It would be easier to try something new than stick with a plan not working.

And now you know the secret. When you take steps physically, mentally, and spiritually, they mix together to create a potion for change unlike any other. Your newfound mental health skills will make healthy eating easier. When your spirit has hope for the future, you will have greater patience in relationships. And a strong body will give you the confidence needed to manage your emotions.

It will take effort to be healthy. It is the only way to move forward.

What step will you take today to get unstuck?

BELIEVE YOU CAN CHANGE

To get unstuck, we must believe we can get there. If we don't believe we can change who we are in a relationship, open our hearts to faith, lose those extra ten pounds, or reach a goal, we won't.

It's absolutely necessary for you to believe it.

Do you believe you can change?

This is the only yes-or-no question in this book. It's a one-word answer. Don't put any explanation around it. Just answer, yes or no.

I once asked a man who suffered from anxiety if he thought he could ever be rid of it. He answered emphatically, "No!" and then launched into the reasons it couldn't be so. His explanations were doing nothing but keeping him anxious and stuck. Until we believe getting to a new, healthy place is possible, we will block the ways to get there.

It can be hard to try something new when all else has failed. Trying for years to love an unlovable spouse can make us hardhearted and believe it's impossible to do so. The belief that it can be done, however, is your only way to freedom.

Start by asking yourself why you *don't* believe change can happen. When we begin to list the reasons, we see they are either excuses or a dependence on someone else to fix our problem. These thoughts paint us into a corner and get us stuck.

What reason do you have for being stuck?

We say over and over what we *can't* do and what we *won't* do. When we say those things and believe we don't have the strength to get unstuck, we render our efforts useless. Many people have told me they could *never* run a marathon. I never believe them. If by running a marathon you could save your child from a lifetime of drug abuse, you'd do it. If you could somehow cure cancer with your effort to the finish line, you'd get it done. You have no idea how strong you are.

This doesn't apply just to physical strength. It also happens with our mental health. It always amazes me how people deal with the most horrendous circumstances and live to tell the story. The challenges are tough, no doubt, but not impossible. The belief in our ability to handle whatever comes our way opens the door for it to be so.

When we practice believing we can change in small areas, it allows us to expand to larger areas. Like a basketball player practices free throws, we can practice being nonjudgmental, grateful, and positive. Take a small step toward getting unstuck by proving to yourself that you can.

Change begins with a belief in our minds. My belief you can get unstuck is undergirded by some core beliefs.

No one can make you feel a certain way; you choose your feelings.

The thoughts in your mind are up to you to control.

Worry is a choice.

How you talk to yourself is extremely powerful.

You must not take what other people say personally.

You must not make assumptions about others.

You are enough.

Each person is entitled to their own opinion.

I have been stuck in so many ways. Stuck waiting for people to be nicer to me. Stuck trying to be liked by everyone I know. Stuck entertaining frightening thoughts of what might happen.

Stuck with worry. Stuck beating myself up in my mind. Stuck making up stories about why people did something. Stuck assuming I know the whole truth without asking. Stuck feeling weak but unwilling to stand up for myself. Stuck believing I was inferior to others. Stuck in sorrow over disagreements.

And all of it was preventable. I created the anguish in my mind. The solution was there; I just didn't take responsibility for it. Now, I ask myself questions and figure out what my next move is, since I am the only one that can affect my life. It's both freeing and difficult. I hold the solutions! Taking control of our beliefs allows us the freedom to deal with anything that comes our way.

This is the point I want you to fully understand. Each of us needs a deep-down commitment to our self. It's the understanding that doing nothing is giving up. Attempts to get unstuck, even if they don't work, are still attempts. Those attempts are you screaming at the circumstances, the pain, and the setbacks saying you are still here, still fighting, and not giving up until you've succeeded.

Our beliefs matter. They matter a lot. They help form our thoughts. They determine the extent of our resolve. They shape our lives. If we don't believe there is a way out of being stuck, we will continue to be stuck. But if we search for answers, we will find them.

To change your behavior and get out of the mud puddle, it will take believing it can happen.

Success

Think about the most successful person you know. Maybe they're a gazillionaire or are loved by many. Think about that person. Do you know how they got there? Do you know how they spend their days? What habits do they have?

People do not become successful without paying a price and

won't stay successful without taking care of themselves. Their success is a by-product of a bunch of healthy habits, one on top of the other, that elevate them to the top.

What habits could lead you to success?

Success demands we are in good working order. If we feel weak and frazzled, we can't be focused and productive. When we feel insignificant, it's impossible to create new ideas that will benefit others. It's not possible to feel exhausted and lousy and show another person love. To be successful, we need to be operating like a well-oiled machine.

When we don't take care of ourselves, not only can we not be successful, but also our family suffers, our coworkers suffer, our friends suffer, our community suffers, and ultimately humankind suffers. We get stuck, and they suffer.

TAKE ACTION

It would be so nice if our problems just disappeared overnight. But they don't.

It takes action to get unstuck. Swallow this reality.

Change is necessary. It's up to you.

What is one teeny-tiny action you could take to get unstuck?

The beginning of this process can only be done by you. Although you may be inspired to change by someone else, the first step is taken by you and you alone. There is no other way. Muster up the courage, plan *one* new action, and go for it.

Taking the necessary first step out of your puddle is love. Love for yourself, love for those around you, and ultimately, love for all humanity. It's only when we live outside the mud puddle that we can offer our gifts to the rest of the world. That may seem grandiose, but it's true! Love yourself first. It's the only way.

Our problems are created *for* us. They are an opportunity to grow and learn. Sometimes, the thing we thought would help does not make things better. If you are suffering from stress, you may think giving yourself a break and calming yourself is the answer. But what may work best for you is a workout. Working up a good sweat will burn off unnecessary energy, get you tired enough to sleep well, and allow you to feel more able to handle the stress.

If you have been stuck for a while, you have developed habits that put you there. It takes about three months to undo a bad habit, so it's important to be patient with yourself. Every person who tries to change a behavior will slip back into old habits. It's important to keep in mind that it's easier to develop a good habit than live with a bad one. Keep at it!

Don't expect perfection out of yourself. Give yourself grace. When we're learning a new behavior, we'll make mistakes, be inefficient, and stumble around a bit while we get acclimated. Expect it. Embrace it. Laugh at it. But whatever you do, don't give up on it!

Let's say you decide to practice love. You decide you will no longer think negatively about others but *always* be loving. About ten minutes later, someone cuts you off in traffic and a word or two slip out of your mouth before you have a chance to think. Oops. Now what do you do?

Don't beat yourself up and overapologize; otherwise it becomes your focus. The fact you caught yourself being unloving is enough. The thought was just there. Now is time for action. Think about love toward the other driver and move on. Next time, you will catch yourself sooner.

If you behaved perfectly, you wouldn't be stuck in the first place. We all do it, and there's no shame. Reward yourself as you change your behavior and get out of the mud puddle that holds you back.

To get unstuck, you will need to take action. You knew that, but now you *really* know it. It's a worthy effort, depends on the belief you can do it, and will involve caring for yourself. This is what it will take.

SUMMARY

In the midst of your journey, remember it is a worthy effort.

Now let's see how to make it easier.

Chapter Nine

CHANGE IS EASIER WITH THE HELP OF OTHERS

As the song goes, we all get by with a little help from our friends. Getting help requires us to be vulnerable and ask for it. As difficult as that may seem, it's the quickest way to get unstuck. Other people can give us many things we can't or won't give ourselves. It is helpful to enlist the help and generosity of our friends.

ENCOURAGEMENT

Something tangible happens when a person shows us encouragement. Our heart flutters, we feel their support, and we know we're not alone. Everything is easier when we receive encouragement.

My husband's face at mile seventeen of the Boston Marathon is seared into my memory. He was waving at me enthusiastically, compassionately, and encouragingly. How could I feel so much in just a few seconds? Wrapped up in his look were the months of listening he endured as I processed the difficulty and excitement of my training. He was full of pride and right there with me. He made my legs lighter by cheering me on with his entire heart and soul. During that demanding time, when my muscles were taxed and my energy level waned, he gave me strength.

Encouragement helps us get unstuck.

Who in your life gives you encouraging words?

Have you ever had someone pay you a compliment that you remembered hours or days later? Their confidence in you can be like a hand extended as you look up from your puddle. Once, after I described a situation to a stranger, they said, "Thanks for sharing." And I thought, *Really? Was that something special?* Their gratefulness told me I had something useful to offer. Even a random comment from a stranger can help us.

Encouraging words can give us the confidence to take a step away from being stuck. It can be just enough fuel to help us. Like a cold glass of water on a hot summer day, it will refresh us and give us what it takes to move forward.

WISDOM

Transformation from our place of stuck can be easier with a well-placed piece of wisdom from someone who has lived through our current circumstances, spent time studying and pondering life's great mysteries, or simply has the gift. It's good to have those people in our lives.

Wisdom can come from the simplest of places. I knew a mentally challenged woman who spoke many pieces of wisdom into my life. Another woman who had struggled immensely through her life told me, "People are tricky," and this wisdom has stayed with me for years. And my eighty-seven-year-old mom with dementia has graced me with pearls of wisdom from a mouth that no longer contains her own teeth.

We need to keep our ears and hearts open to the wisdom all around us.

Where is an unexpected place to find wisdom?

Imagine a person standing on the sidewalk handing out hundred-dollar bills. We could walk right by and not take one, but that would be silly! We could take the bill, look at it, turn it over in our hands, and then let it fall to the ground. That would be foolish! Or we could take that hundred dollars and use it for our benefit.

Wisdom is the same way.

COACH

We all need to be challenged by a coach now and then to get unstuck. It can be something as simple as a math problem we can't figure out or as complex as whether to continue a relationship. A well-qualified parent, teacher, coach, or mentor can give us that kick in the pants and help move us out of the mud puddle and on our way.

CHANGING LIVES

I took beginner-level swim lessons six times. It wasn't due to poor instruction or my lack of talent but my fear of the deep water from my near-drowning experience. Each time we were asked to swim through the deep water, I snuck off to avoid my fear.

On my sixth go of it, the lessons were held at our junior high's indoor swimming pool. The teacher, Mr. Luke, was on to me. We were instructed to line up at the diving well, where the water plummeted to nine feet deep. I made my getaway by sneaking toward the locker room. But Mr. Luke had a plan. The door was locked. I clung to the big silver handle crying and shaking. His resolve was softened by the fear in my eyes. He pulled out a key ring that seemed to hold a thousand keys, unlocked the door, and let me escape to the safety of the girl's locker room.

My parent's concern one of their children would drown in one of Minnesota's ten thousand lakes called for desperate measures. They arranged for a private lesson at the lake I had almost drowned in with none other than Mr. Luke. He put on his friendliest gold-crowned grin, got me in the water, and said, "Just lie on your back, Cathy. We'll walk around a bit." Before I knew it, he had taken me out to the big dock where there was nothing but deep-green water between me and the safety of the sandy beach.

"You're going to swim back," instructed Mr. Luke.

I pleaded with him, "Will you swim with me?" He grinned and nodded. With Mr. Luke beside me, I dog-paddled through my fear, keeping him in my sight.

That day changed my life.

Shortly after, I began to swim competitively, and in high school, Mr. Luke became my coach. Had I not been challenged by Mr. Luke, my life would have been different. I would never have understood I was an athlete, developed the confidence that swimming gave me, and enjoyed a lifetime sport that fuels my soul.

Later in my life, I was fortunate enough to see Mr. Luke again. When I called to arrange a time to meet, he said, "I won't lock the door on you!" As it turned out, the challenge of getting me over my fear had changed his life too. He told the story often as a testament to his persistence and desire to get children to love the water and learn to swim.

Mr. Luke got me unstuck and introduced me to a lifetime of opportunity. It wouldn't have happened without him.

Sometimes we need to be challenged by someone else to get unstuck from the difficulties in our lives.

What have others been challenging you to as a way out?

THE POWER IS IN YOU

"In the event of a sudden loss in air pressure, an oxygen mask will automatically appear in front of you. . . . If you are traveling with someone who requires assistance . . . secure your mask first, and then assist the other person."

If you've ever flown, this will sound familiar. I remember being surprised the first time I heard it. Secure your mask first? Won't the person requiring assistance die, choke, suffocate, or freak out if I don't tend to them first?

You'll both die if you don't do it in that order. Take care of yourself first; then, and only then, can you assist others. The airline industry knows it, and now you do too.

Although it will be easier to get unstuck with the help of others, the work comes down to you. It always does.

Look within.

This is why I wrote a self-help book. It may be why there are so many of them out there. People have discovered it comes down to them. It always does. I needed to help myself.

My journey was no more difficult or arduous than yours. What I learned as I struggled to get out of my mud puddle was the power in getting strong physically, mentally, and spiritually. Together, these three have the power to move anyone forward on their journey. They interact with each other in magnificent ways.

When faced with a problem, I can get the best advice in the world, but no one can put on running shoes and get me into shape. No one can eat right for me. And I am the one who must put on my jammies and get enough sleep.

There is no way another person can make a decision for me to connect with others, think positively to myself, or establish personal boundaries. Only I can own my emotions and will myself to live intentionally. It comes down to me. It always does.

I can go to church and follow all the rules, but no one else can change my heart. No one can love for me; I must do it myself. Gratitude is something only I can practice for myself. The meaning of life events is unique. No one else can determine them for me. No one else can determine my purpose and carry it out. It comes down to me. It always does.

Here is the good news: We each have the power within us to carry this out. There are steps each of us can take to improve our lives. Each of us lives in a body that needs to be cared for. Each of us has a mind and has enormous potential to expand it. Each of us has a spirit with unlimited potential for love.

The power is in you.

Section Three

HOW TO GET UNSTUCK

You've got the power, but how do you access it? What steps do you take? Where do you start? Although this can seem overwhelming, it does not need to be. You're stuck now, and you are making it day to day. All you need to do is take a step away from an unhealthy habit that is making your life difficult.

To make a change, you're going to have to take a step. Before you start the excuses, engage in negative self-talk, and hang your head low, just take a small step. Any step will do. Some will be easier for you and some will be hard. It's always that way.

I exercise a lot. Many of you can't believe I can have so much discipline. But look at yourself: some of you have lots of friends, and it's hard for me to believe that comes so naturally for you. Do you see the difference? What's difficult for me is easy for you. What's easy for me is difficult for you. We're all just made differently yet are so much the same.

Everyone has a body, mind, and spirit. All three areas must be in good working order to get unstuck. For some people, taking care of their body will be the most difficult part of this process. For others, caring for their spirit will seem unnatural and cumbersome. The key is pursuing wellness in all three areas. Sometimes it will be hard, and sometimes it will be easy.

How will you access your power? By improving how your body, mind, and spirit operate. What steps will you take? The ones you need to. Your plan will be different than anyone else's. Look at where you're stuck, what has gotten you there, and what needs to be improved to get out. Is it a lack of self-care? Unchecked feelings? Outdated beliefs? Personal boundaries? A habit of ungratefulness?

The motivation will be up to you. It's your body, your mind, your spirit, and your life. No one will care about it as much as you. Others can inspire and encourage, but the work is up to you. Every human being on the planet is in the same predicament. Your life is your own, and it's up to you to manage it. Either you are motivated to make it the best it can be, or you take the course set out by the circumstances and whims of those around you.

How do you get unstuck? Be committed to yourself. Love yourself more than anyone else does. Take a step forward to be free.

Chapter Ten

FREE YOUR BODY

One of the things that make humans unique is our ability to use tools. We drive cars to get from point A to point B; we use computers to communicate and calculate; we use hammers and levels to build a wall.

But imagine trying to use a computer to build a wall, or to use a car to do long division. Each tool has its own use. In addition, our tools need to be primed for the job we ask of them.

Have you ever tried to cut something with a dull knife? It will make the job harder than necessary. But when knives are sharpened, they'll cut through food without pushing too hard and slipping. When we're trying to get unstuck, we need to make sure we've got the right tool for the job.

Take a Good Look

Take a look at yourself in the mirror. Imagine you could grab your hips, pull your whole body over your head, and set it next to you. Take a look at it. It's just your body. Think of it as a tool. It needs to be fed, moved, and given rest in order to perform well.

There it stands, unable to care for itself. It will take our mind and heart to give the body what it needs to perform well. It needs to eat right. Just like a car needs gasoline or electricity to run, our body needs the right fuel. Putting ketchup in the gas tank of a car will ruin the engine, and it won't move. Our body needs the right fuel at the right time to produce the best results and feel good.

And our body will also need to move. It needs to stay active to avoid getting sluggish and tired. Take another look at the body standing next to you. It can't move on its own. It will need to be cared for by our mind and heart. Like an engine, maintaining its moving parts will cause it to run like a well-oiled machine. It's a very effective tool when it's taken care of.

And our body will need to rest. It's not capable of running 24/7. Regardless of how special or unique we think we are, our body must rest. It's created this way. Pushing it too hard or long will cause wear and tear.

Just like we would care for an infant—making sure they get fed, allowing them to play, and putting them down for a nap—we must care for our body. Look at your body one last time standing next to you. It deserves your love and needs your care. It's the only body you have. You live in it every single day.

We get stuck when our body is unhealthy, so we must heal from what's ailing us. The only way to heal our body is to care for it. As we work to strengthen our body, it will heal. Only then will it be free.

Feed Your Body

You are what you eat. It was a popular saying in the seventies, and it's still true.

But what are we supposed to eat? Is fat good or bad for us? Carbs or no carbs? Do we need to take supplements? Many people throw up their hands in frustration. I get it. Let's talk about three different parts of this that will help you to navigate these tricky waters.

First of all, it's our responsibility to eat right. It's not the surgeon general's, Dr. Oz's, or our spouse's. If we get sick because our immune system is weak, the surgeon general isn't going to suffer; we are. We are the one who feels the pain. We are the ones who must call in sick to work, miss the birthday party, or drag ourselves to a can't-miss event.

When we eat right, food fuels our body in amazing ways. We have more energy, feel more alert, and have a more positive attitude. We'll jump higher and sleep better.

As adults, we make our own food choices. We grocery shop or pick something from a menu. We cook or bake and then put all the deliciousness into our mouths. We get to choose.

How do you choose what to eat?

I hear some of you saying, "Yeah, but . . . the dorm food is so starchy, I don't have time to eat right, I just can't pass up a piece of chocolate cake, I didn't want to hurt her feelings by not having one of her lemon bars, there was no other option but McWhatever on our road trip, I was *so* hungry I had to eat whatever I could get . . ." Blah blah blah.

Each of those statements is really saying, "I didn't plan ahead," "I don't believe what I eat is important," or, "I'm leaving it up to someone else to decide what I ingest." Gulp.

If you're allergic to nuts, you'll do whatever it takes to stay away from nuts. You'll ask awkward questions, say *no thank you*, or bring your own food so you don't end up drinking a bottle of Benadryl and going to the ER. It's nonnegotiable.

We need to have the same mindset about what we eat. It's our responsibility. No one else will monitor our caloric intake and cut us off. No one will force us to eat our peas like our mom may have done when we were a child. No one will slap our hand as we reach for the second piece of pie. It's our responsibility.

On a scale of one to ten, how responsible are you for your food choices? Why?

Are you making your food choices based on what other people are doing? It would be a better idea to pay attention to how you feel with what you eat. Although most of America is drinking three cups of coffee a day just to stay normal, I become Mr. Hyde when I get jacked up on caffeine. Because I'm not like most of America, I can't drink caffeine like almost everyone else.

Recently, we've discovered that people can be sensitive to all kinds of foods, including gluten, dairy, and sugar. It can be hard for you to believe it if those foods don't affect you in a negative way. What underlies the confusion is that we want to all belong to the same camp and have others think (and eat) just like us.

But we're all different. Each of our bodies has basically the same functions, but they are infinitely complex. Some people can eat lots of food and not gain weight, while others struggle if they look at a piece of chocolate out of the corner of their eye. Some like the heat and others prefer cold. Some wake up energetic in the morning and others gain steam at the end of the day. Our bodies function differently, and we need to let the comparisons go, stop the jealousy, and focus on our own diet.

What foods do you feel good after eating?

What foods do you feel bad after eating?

Each year, scientists discover more about how food affects our bodies. We're not done learning yet! As our environment changes, as we better understand how our genes shut on and off, and as our culture changes, we will need to change and adapt what and how we eat. This is something each of us needs to discover for ourselves.

As our bodies age, they also require more and less of different foods. We can't eat baby food our whole lives, nor can we down copious amounts of beer and pizza at age fifty and feel anywhere near normal the next day. We need to be continuous learners and adapt our diet to our ever-changing body.

Our planet has changed too. We have new foods available (who knew about quinoa in 1990?) that may or may not be good for us. Companies package foods differently with tempting new marketing ploys to change our thinking. Frosted Flakes are now marketed as a healthy way for a kid to start the day, but when I was a kid they were called Sugar Frosted Flakes and were marketed based on their taste. And government policy sets the direction of prices and availability of foods. We need to stay in the game and figure out what works for our body.

How has your eating changed over time?

It's our responsibility to eat right. Not what the neighbor is eating, but what we know our body needs. Not what we ate ten years ago, but what current thought and science have discovered.

When we begin to eat right, we begin to control our body. For some people, this can be very empowering. Each bite is more than an instant reward; it's an investment in your biggest asset. You show yourself you matter. It's love.

We all must eat, and ultimately the control is ours. Eating a balanced diet that fuels our body and mind will give us the energy it takes to get unstuck. Not doing so will lead us to unhealthy places because our bodies need fuel.

It's easy to see in children. When they haven't eaten, they get cranky. If they've had too much sugar, they're overactive. Some children have an emotional meltdown because they're allergic to foods. Their little bodies have big reactions to what they eat.

Many adults get this way too. But we don't always draw the connection between how we feel and what we've eaten. Intuitively, we know what food does for us. This is why we reach for comfort food when we're sad. But when we're agitated, we don't stop and think, "Did I have breakfast? Have I had too much caffeine?" When sleepy, we rarely ask, "Did I overload with carbs? When was the last time I ate? Have I been consuming a lot of sugar?"

Foods have all kinds of effects on our mood. Some people can work through a day without taking time to eat anything. But even though their stomach doesn't growl or get uncomfortable, their mood becomes gloomy. Even the most positive person can be in distress because of their lack of calories.

Each person can come up with their own "recipe" of what combination of foods works for them based on the strengths of their body, time of life, activity level, illness, and stress. There are certainly rules of thumb, but each of us must figure it out for ourselves.

Every day, things change. Stress, the weather, activity, age, and challenges alter what our body needs. It's not a one-and-done solution. Determining the best foods for us will be a lifelong journey as both our body and the world change. What we eat will affect how we feel about our life. The point is everything we put in our mouth will affect how our body feels and, therefore, affect our emotions. Pay attention.

My body is like a demanding toddler. She gets hungry, tired, cold, hot, or fidgety and screams out her complaint. She leaves me unmotivated, sleepy, searching for a warm place to hide or opening the refrigerator door to cool off. When she's hurt, she'll cause me to focus on the immediate need of how to get relief.

It's just like living with a two-year-old.

Caring for my body by being intentional about what I eat is essential to my feeling good. It's the same for you. Work on yourself and figure out what gets you to the most energetic, focused, and positive person you can be. Study your food choices. There is a lot to be learned by paying attention. Food is medicine, and we need to treat it that way.

What emotional changes can you tie to eating a certain food?

What foods give you extra energy?

MOVE YOUR BODY

We were created to move. Watch a toddler all day and you'll see how natural it is for them to stay in motion. Watch an ant, a squirrel, or a dog. They don't stop unless they are eating or sleeping.

We need to move too. It's being said that sitting is the new smoking. Standing desks are all the rage. Fitness trackers are becoming commonplace. And we're getting our kids to get out from behind their technology to go outside and play. We as a society are realizing the pendulum has shifted too far to the side of sedentary, and we need to settle into a more active routine.

Advances in so many areas of our lives, however, have made it less necessary to be constantly in motion. The TV remote allows us to stay in our recliner as we peruse almost endless choices of what to watch. Amazon delivers almost anything we could shop for right to our doorstep. And a digital assistant will answer our questions and help with tasks without us even picking up our smartphone.

On top of all the technology that reduces our movement, many of us sit at desks and work long hours, finding no time to stroll in the park. We jump in our cars and go from here to there, stopping at the drive-through to pick up dinner in an effort to race home and collapse on the couch. The thought of walking a mile or two each day seems crazy and doesn't fit our lifestyle.

What are we to do?

The problem isn't exercise or your good intentions. The problem is the method. When we start too fast, we need to stop and catch our breath because it's simply not sustainable.

We've all had grand aspirations that have been impossible to keep. We want to lose weight, learn a new skill, or exercise. These are all attainable, but we dive in too fast and too deep and then need to come up for air. We decide to exercise five days a week for one hour at a time. After day two, we are achy and tired. We force ourselves to exercise on day three but then give up because it's just too hard.

It's like the old joke: How do you eat an elephant? One bite at a time.

What small step could you take to move your body more?

Our bodies were meant to move. When we exercise, endorphins are released, causing us to feel good. Exercise also tones the body, leading to improved self-esteem. The act of exercise reduces stress and helps us sleep better.

It's also believed that, when we walk, our creativity can be released. The simple act of moving our bodies and clearing our minds allows us to come up with thoughts we can't force out in front of a computer screen. This has happened many times with me. The act of intentionally freeing our mind allows it to wander to inspired thoughts.

THE HALF MARATHON

At age fifty-one, I decided to run a half marathon. Admittedly, it was naïve and a little arrogant. I had not exercised in twenty-five years.

I began by running by myself, and eventually joined a group that ran on Saturdays. It was fun to be with others on their journey to the finish line. My self-esteem grew with each passing mile. I began to prove to myself I could go a few more miles, even though it was difficult. Week by week, my legs grew a little stronger.

On the day of the race, the racers were crammed into the starting shoot. The national anthem played loudly on huge speakers. As I looked around, I saw other nervous faces like mine and some surprisingly calm and happy ones. The gun sounded, and we were off.

As we settled into mile two, all I could hear was the sound of shoes on the pavement. It was so peaceful. I felt calm and happy to be there too, part of a pack of people ready to stretch themselves that day.

At mile ten, my energy began to fade. My mind got fuzzy, and I wanted to quit. It was as if someone came in and shut off the lights. I stumbled up to a volunteer who cheerfully handed me a Dixie cup of ice. I grabbed it and shoved it into my mouth. Chewing on the ice was like magic. Suddenly I had more energy and my mind came back to a sunny place.

Another two miles closer to the finish, my energy again

dropped into the toilet. I ran by a young woman who had been in front of me the whole time. She was a cute twentysomething in a darling tie-dyed T-shirt that matched her friend's. I wanted her to finish! If I could do this, she could too. By then she had slowed to a walk, with her shoulders hunched in a defeated position. "Come on, we've only got a little bit more to go!" I said, surprising both her and me.

As if swallowing another drop of magic, my mood shot up from a three to a ten. The simple act of being in this with someone else, even a perfect stranger, and giving them a small bit of encouragement changed my perspective. She looked surprised and started to run again.

Thinking about the end of the race still chokes me up. I ran across the finish line and felt more empowered than any other time in my life. I did it. A fifty-one-year-old woman who had done nothing but be anxious and depressed her whole life. Until that moment, I wasn't sure I could do it. I was grateful and surprised, exhausted and happy.

I finished not because I was more fit than the next person, because I certainly was not! It wasn't because I had more willpower than others. Nor was it because I had more money or time. I finished because I wanted to, and I took a step. I was inspired by other people I saw doing it and decided I would try.

I wasn't too old to get unstuck, and neither are you.

Movement became my new friend. She makes me feel amazing and strong, capable and challenged. She kicks my butt and has brought me to the most amazing places. She's a necessary companion, and we can either get along or be in constant disharmony.

Movement is within each one of us, just waiting to come out. Take her hand and embrace the challenge. How will you do it? Dancing, walking, gardening, skiing, hiking, rowing, swimming, biking, yoga, weight-lifting, playing basketball, jumping, cartwheeling, hula-hooping, or climbing a mountain—whatever it is, take her hand. There's nothing to be afraid of! This is how you were created. And it's freeing.

We need movement to feel physically, mentally, and spiritually well. It must be a priority in our life if we want to get unstuck.

We must move.

REST YOUR BODY

After a day of movement, we need to rest.

Let's talk about sleep. We all need to do it. Without it, we can't function properly. It's a precious commodity, and so many things assault this area of our lives. To get unstuck and stay there, we must get serious about our sleep and protect it like a precious diamond.

SAYING NO

When I think about my life, one principle has emerged as reasonable and true. I was not put on this earth to run around like a chicken with my head cut off. Seriously. Looking at some of the most influential people throughout history, I see many stories of staying focused on a purpose despite obstacles. I also look at people who I see as accomplishing a lot with their lives today. A principle that shines is their ability to say no to things. They are focused on a few things instead of being pulled every which way toward things not useful for what they are striving for. It's a good idea to say no to the good and yes to the great.

What does this have to do with sleep? To accomplish anything great, we need to be at our best. To be at our best, we need to get enough sleep. It must be a priority. We need to take it seriously and protect it.

On average, Americans have seven different lights on in their bedroom at night. Think about the light from your phone, TV, DVD player, computer, alarm clock, or smartwatch—not to mention the lights coming in from outside. We need to have it as dark as possible for our bodies to get a good night's sleep. If you must, wear sleeping blinders.

We're in a competitive, busy, and distracted culture. There are twenty-four-hour news channels, social media, entire series available with a click, and text messages that can demand our immediate attention. We try to do more in a day than is possible. We say yes to things we don't have time for. We have not built any margin into our lives for the inevitable surprises life throws at us. All these press on the hours we need for sleep.

How much sleep would it take for you to feel rested each morning?

We need to get enough sleep. But how much is enough? Nine out of ten people need between seven and nine hours per night. Interestingly, professional athletes, musicians, chess players, and actors get on average eight hours and thirty-six minutes of sleep a night. That is an hour and a half more than the average American.

Maybe that's why they're professionals.

Here's a way to figure out if you're getting enough sleep. If you wake with an alarm and feel sleepy, try going to bed fifteen minutes earlier. If you're still sleepy in the morning, try going to bed thirty minutes earlier. Eventually, you will find the amount of sleep you need to wake refreshed.

Wouldn't it be great to wake up refreshed every day?

I hear you giving me a "Yeah, but . . . the kids, the husband, the cookies that need to be baked, the costume that needs to be sewn, the toys that need to be picked up, the teenager who isn't even home yet!" All those problems have solutions. In a busy household, it will happen easier if everyone is on the same page. Have a discussion about sleep. Brainstorm ideas to help each person get enough. Talk about how you feel when you get enough sleep and when you don't.

It's important not to allow children to dictate sleep patterns that we know are bad for them. Our kids were constantly invited to sleepovers, which I argued were not sleepovers at all because no one slept. They were all-night parties that created grumpy little monsters who were good for nothing the next day. They weren't bad children. They were just reacting to the lack of what their little bodies needed.

Another difficulty is teenagers who stay up late staring at screens and then need to sleep later in the mornings to feel human. Screaming, "Go to bed!" doesn't work. (I've tried it.) Having a family discussion about the value of sleep and all its benefits is a better tactic. When their bodies are growing, children have an even greater need to get an adequate amount of sleep. The teenage years are difficult enough. Don't make it harder for them by not protecting their sleep. It's likely they'll get stuck if they're sleep deprived, just like you.

It's loving to teach our children to get enough sleep and protect it for them until they believe it themselves.

Our American culture has a distorted belief about getting by on a few hours of sleep a night. We believe it indicates a person is somehow stronger or more resilient than the rest of us. It's as if we're competing and the one who gets the least sleep wins. People puff out their chest to show how *strong* they are. They lead us to believe they get way more done and are some kind of unique human being, built like no other.

How does sleep affect you?

Take some time to ponder the questions below. Close your eyes, see yourself in the situation, and recall the feelings you had. Take a moment to go back there. This exercise will help you figure out if you've been at your best or worst due to your sleep patterns.

Think about the last strenuous physical activity you engaged in. Were you well rested? Did it matter? Would it have helped if you had slept more before you faced the challenge?

Think about the last difficult mental challenge you had. Maybe it was a test or a challenging conversation. Were you well rested before you had it? In hindsight, would you have acted better if you had been more rested?

Think about a recent spiritual challenge. Maybe you lost hope in your dreams or suffered a loss of love. Were you well rested before it happened? Can you imagine how you would have felt if you had been energized and strong in your body? Somber thoughts will always seem better after a good night's sleep.

We often don't think of sleep as a critical component in the quality of our life. But it is. And it's so easy to improve! Recognizing its power is a life hack.

What step will you take to ensure you get adequate sleep tonight?

Getting adequate sleep is essential to living a happy and productive life. Working on getting more of it is just like hitting the gym four times a week to build muscle. But doesn't it seem a little easier? Maybe this is the first thing you begin to work on to improve your life.

Summary

Feeding, moving, and resting our body frees it to be at its best. In this freedom come strength, flexibility, and resilience. We will feel energetic, which leads to optimism. Strong body parts keep us from illness and allow us to feel good. Flexibility matters as we go through life and can maintain our balance, do the activities we want to engage in, and avoid sore muscles with new movements.

But it's not just physical. Caring for our body will also give us mental and spiritual strength. It will allow us to be mentally flexible and spiritually strong. And a well-cared-for body is resilient to life's curveballs and changing norms. A body tended to on a consistent basis is free. It serves as a useful and magnificent tool instead of a source of pain and discomfort.

Our bodies are really quite amazing tools and are the foundation for a great life. When we see them as such, we'll be kind to them. We'll understand their value and purpose. They simply package our heart and mind, the essence of who we are. They're necessary, however, for carrying out our life.

Free your body. Free your life.

Taking care of our body is just one of the ways we can get unstuck.

Chapter Eleven
FREE YOUR MIND

Another way to get unstuck and have a happier and more productive life is to free our mind. When I struggled with depression, this was hard, not so much because of what it took to free my mind but because I didn't have the knowledge or skills to do it.

Freeing our minds is just like learning any new skill. It will take knowledge, understanding, and practice. It is possible. It can be done.

Mental health skills are not mystical or complicated. Most often, however, we don't realize how our thinking is skewed because we don't speak those nasty thoughts out loud. We believe everyone else thinks the same way we do, having the false notion we have nothing new to learn about relating with others and ourselves. Are mental health skills difficult to develop? Maybe at first. But just like anything, working on them is easier every day. And when we realize how we're suffering because we're not employing them, it becomes obvious that the benefits of a healthy mental life will far outweigh the relatively small amount of effort to get there.

There are four basic areas to freeing our minds. Because we're created as social beings, we must connect with others. We also must connect with ourselves in a healthy way. Where the two meet, we must have healthy personal boundaries so that each person is clear about who the other person is. And lastly, we need to take ownership of our life.

You may notice this has more to do with you than others. This is good news because we are the only ones we can change.

Mental health is critical to getting and staying unstuck. These principles need to be at the forefront of our minds as we walk through life encountering conflict, stress, doubt, and people. As we understand our own motivations and stop making up stories about theirs, we'll be free to love our lives.

We get stuck when our mind is unhealthy, so we must heal from what's ailing us. The only way to heal our mind is to care for it. As we work to strengthen our mind, it will heal. Only then will it be free. It's up to us.

CONNECT WITH OTHERS

> *When one tugs at a single thing in nature,*
> *he finds it attached to the rest of the world.*
>
> —*John Muir*

We're social beings. This is a social universe. All things are connected to one another.

A recent study at Brigham Young University suggested social isolation and loneliness kill more people than obesity. A Harvard study of over seventy years determined the number-one factor in how well we age is how connected we are to others. A major tenet to our mental health is our relationships with others.

We need deep and meaningful relationships to thrive in our lives. Our culture, however, undermines these important connections with others. This fast-paced world pushes us to accomplish more tasks and spend less time socializing. Technology allows us to connect virtually instead of physically. Although we may seem more connected than ever, we are more isolated, and this is having a negative impact on our mental health.

People are entering assisted living and memory-care units at record numbers in their final years of life. To help them live longer and more happily, this industry has designed the facilities around community. Bedrooms are small, and residents are encouraged to spend time in the common living areas and eat together. This is the best way to help them age well.

How do you engage with others on a weekly basis?

Dr. Caroline Leaf, a noted neurological scientist, believes we are all wired for love. She has these suggestions to combat the effects of loneliness: have meaningful discussions, volunteer, turn off your smartphone, get out of the house, be friendly to others, and reach out for help.

There's a sense of relief when we're with others. We breathe a little easier. When we're with others, we get out of our own head and focus outside ourselves. People distract us from our current struggles, blasting our lives with a dose of theirs. It's a wonderful potion.

Even sitting in a waiting room by yourself is not as pleasant as sitting in the same room with others. Even if we're not speaking to one another, we feel somehow connected when another human being is present. We casually glance up from our magazine and wonder what they're here for. We wonder how old they are, if we'll ever see them again, and if they're happy. We're connected.

When we're with others, we're forced to stop thinking about ourselves. At a lively party, the distractions are constant. At work, we engage with others to get our tasks done. At home, we hear from others and see them as they move around. We're aware of them. This causes a part of our mind to think about them, care about them, or embrace them. It takes us away from purely introspective thoughts.

I'm an introvert. It's easier to curl up with a book than go to the party. But we are designed to connect with others. It is good for us and we need it. We do need interaction with others to have a full and healthy life. If you're an introvert like me, this may feel like a struggle, but like most things, it will get easier over time. Remember, everyone has a few things that are critical to their health but difficult for them to do. This might be yours. Put on a smile and get out there.

Being with others gives us a broader perspective. Every person has a unique set of circumstances that have shaped their lives. When we hear from others, our world expands. Even though we may not agree with what others say, simply hearing varying perspectives expands our own.

Importantly, when we engage with others, we have someone to share our troubles with. Very rarely can we see our struggles objectively, and we usually need insight from friends to help us sort it out. Asking for help is a beautiful and fast way to get unstuck.

And when we have others in our lives, we can rejoice together. It's way more fun to celebrate your birthday with friends than alone. We laugh when we're with others much more than we laugh alone. It's more fun to hug a friend on their recent success than send a card. And it's more fun to run a marathon with other competitors than by yourself. We need to gather. We need community. We need a place among others. We were designed this way.

*How do you satisfy your need to
be connected with others?*

CONNECT WITH SELF

In addition to connecting with others, we need to have a healthy connection with our self. What we think and say about ourselves is important for freeing our mind.

To be healthy and unstuck, it's crucial to know how to keep your thoughts positive. This is easier for some people than others. Some more naturally see the glass as half full rather than half empty. Others might envision themselves as positive thinkers, but upon closer examination, their world is filled with more gloom than gladness.

Let's define self-talk. Positive self-talk is anything you say to yourself that causes you to feel happy, glad, joyful, empowered, strong, hopeful, content, peaceful, loving, important, or motivated. Negative self-talk is the opposite and causes you to feel sad, angry, cynical, weak, agitated, anxious, nervous, fearful, unimportant, or stuck.

Learning how to have positive self-talk was a major turning point in getting me out of my depressed state. Once I realized how many negative thoughts were in my mind and the damage they were doing, I was able to quickly change, and it improved my life dramatically.

Are your thoughts primarily positive or negative?

Think about the thoughts in your mind right now. This can feel a little weird— but, trust me, it's a skill you're going to want to hone. Imagine hiding behind yourself and listening to you say the thoughts in your mind out loud. Are you embarrassed? Joyful? Do you want to get away from her because she's a Debbie Downer?

When I was depressed, my negative thoughts stayed inside my head, and I believed I was a fairly positive person. As a part of some cognitive behavior therapy, I was instructed to carry around a small notebook. On the left-hand side of the page, I would write any negative thoughts that came into my mind. On the right-hand side, I would rephrase the thought in a positive way.

Often, rephrasing the thought was more about taking out the hyperbole and speaking the truth. Instead of "I'm the worst mom in the world!" I would say, "I'm a mom and I love my kids." Instead of "He always misunderstands me!" I would say, "We don't understand each other. Let's see if we can get on the same page."

This simple exercise taught me how to catch my negative thoughts. Suddenly I became very aware of what the person I was hiding behind was saying. This had to stop! I realized how destructive all these negative thoughts were for my mind, body, and soul.

If you lived with someone who constantly spewed negative comments about your dress, your coworkers, and your life, you'd want to stop living with them. The problem is, we can't stop living with ourselves. With our own thoughts, we can subject ourselves to a kind of misery we would never want to inflict on anyone else.

Using extreme words is a sign of extreme thinking. Extreme thinking isn't the truth; it's blown up in either a positive or negative direction. As I mentioned earlier, teenagers often do it for effect. They use extreme language when they're unsure or uncomfortable with what they're saying. If you find yourself using the words *always, never, a million, don't, can't, should,* or *shouldn't,* watch out! Ask yourself if it's really *always* or *never.* Bring your thinking back to the truth and rephrase it as such.

To practice, take a walk and say positive things about everything you observe. If this is a chore, you can be sure you have a habit of negative thinking. Use a fifteen-minute walk to recognize the beautiful flowers and not the ugly house. Be grateful that you can get outside instead of grumbling about the weather. Look for things that can be complimented instead of letting your mind float to all you don't like.

Perfectionism is the root of a lot of negative thinking. When I'm striving for perfection, I become judgmental. Everyone is a rival or someone to compare myself to. Do you see how self-centered this is? It leads to negative thinking.

The good news about negative self-talk is it's just a bad habit. Habits can be learned, and they can also be unlearned. Your negative self-talk can turn into positive self-talk. I know this is true because I did it. It was a total game-changer. Before long, I could hear my negative thoughts, walk them to the curb, and shut the gate behind them.

It wasn't hard to change my negative thinking habit because I realized how destructive it was. It was ruining me from the inside. I learned quickly how to rephrase a negative thought into a truthful or positive one. This felt so much better!

Do you have a friend you wish were by your side day and night to cheer you up? She always has a positive comment to whatever comes her way. She easily laughs off people's quirks, not to judge them but simply to let them be themselves. She easily joins a conversation, not to monopolize but to participate. Her healthy sense of self makes her a joy to be around. You can be that person.

You also have the power to cheer yourself up at any time of the day or night. Remember all those thoughts in your head?

Have a positive conversation with yourself! Give yourself a pep talk like you would if a friend came to you and was sad. Give encouraging words to yourself, just like you would to someone else who desperately needed them. Close your eyes and remember the coolest place you've been. Smell it. Feel it. Let your heart soar like it did then. Poof, you're cheered up!

Words, both spoken and unspoken, have power. They can be revolutionary, destructive, or simply a waste of time. Pay attention to the words in your mind, and use them for your benefit. Being in a positive state of mind will flow to those around you. A smile will show up on your face and then on theirs.

Positive self-talk is a healthy mental health habit. Use it to free your mind and get unstuck.

What can you do to improve your mental life?

Where the Two Meet

Now that we are connecting with others and have a good sense of ourselves, it's time to figure out what happens when the two meet. How will we navigate the eventual conflicts as they arise? To have good mental health, we need skills to help us when struggles arrive.

If people understood personal boundaries, everyone's life would be better. When you understand personal boundaries, you can navigate difficult relationships by understanding both what you're responsible and what you're not responsible for.

People are tricky. Although I first laughed at this simple truth, it continues to help me understand people whom I disagree with. The reason people are tricky is that we are all completely unique. We're born into a family only our siblings share. We have a lifetime of experiences unique to us. We have different faith traditions, expectations, and beliefs. We look different, and people respond to us in different ways. We have separate motivations and goals. The combination of these differences opens the door for confusion.

Our differences also lead to conflict. We misunderstand one another, fill in the blanks when we don't know the whole story, and let fear take over uncertainty. Understanding boundaries shows us how to separate what is me and what is not me. Conflicts subside when we stop trying to control what isn't ours to control.

When we play games, we follow the rules. They let everyone know what to expect and what can and cannot be done. When playing Crazy Eights, nines are not wild. When playing Monopoly, you know what to do when you pick the "Go Directly to Jail" card. In a race, you can't start running before the gun goes off.

There are rules in relationships too, but we each have slightly different versions of them. Things turn chaotic when we don't understand each other's rules. Suddenly there is blame, shame, guilt, and hurt feelings. We're confused with the words and actions of others because we're playing by different rules than they are.

Unfortunately, the only rules we can enforce in relationships are the ones on ourselves. This is where personal boundaries come into play. When we take responsibility for ourselves, communicate clearly to others what we want, and stay consistent, all our relationships will be better.

Boundaries are best explained by using a physical example. Let's create an image in our minds to represent our lives, using physical aspects to represent different parts we're responsible for. Imagine your life as a yard. It stretches out in front of you. Everything in this yard is yours and yours alone.

The weather is perfect. What is perfect weather to you? Feel it.

You sit in a chair. Imagine how comfortable you are in that position. Breathe deeply. You're relaxed and happy.

In your hand, you hold your favorite beverage. Taste it. Mmmmmm.

As you look out at your yard, there is something beautiful in it. My yard has lilac bushes, but yours can have a souped-up Harley or a piece of fine art. Picture in your mind what holds beauty for you.

Around your yard is a beautiful fence. What does it look like?

Now imagine, on the outside of the fence, something all the neighbors enjoy. Maybe there are beautiful flowers or a climbing wall. It could be that you have picnic tables with fresh fruit or a blank canvas with paints.

Finally, in the fence is a gate. Envision it.

Imagine what your yard looks like.

Each of these elements represents something in your life that is your responsibility to care for. Keeping these in mind will help define what you can take care of to have better personal boundaries.

WEATHER

The weather in your imaginary yard represents your emotions. We all have them. Just like the weather changes, sometimes our emotions seem to pop out of nowhere and derail our thoughts. Other times our emotions add extra pleasure to our activities. Either way, our emotions are ours to handle.

My emotions used to be my biggest enemy. I was sad so much of the time, and anger erupted many times a day. Life was out of control because my emotions ruled.

Freedom from my powerful emotions came when I realized they were a signal of something inside myself that needed adjusting. This helped me see them as something I was in control of, like the imaginary weather in my yard. I could no longer blame anyone else for my hurt feelings. Those were mine to manage.

Once I stopped blaming others for my bad feelings, I was forced to look to myself to fix them. I created in my mind the image of a perfect life, and I worked toward choosing emotions that would benefit me. By asking myself reflective questions, I was able to see why certain things bothered me and allowed me to get unstuck from them.

How are you managing the emotions in your life?

CHAIR

The chair you are sitting in represents your attitude. It's the place you choose to sit. Like emotions, no one is responsible for it other than us. Each day is an opportunity to choose your attitude.

Our attitude is our intention. It's what we decide when we wake up in the morning. It's what we say to ourselves before a big meeting. It's the anticipation we feel before dinner with friends. What is your attitude?

What thoughts are in your mind before a trip? Are you excited at the prospect of visiting a new place or anxious about the arrangements? How about a new job? Are you looking forward to new challenges or nervous you may not make a good impression? How about seeing an old friend? Are you anticipating a good conversation or bad?

Our attitude will determine the outcome of the vacation. Fretting over trip arrangements will put you on edge. You can miss the joy in the moment because you've decided to be nervous. The truth is, anticipating trouble will do nothing but steal your joy in the moment.

It's the same with starting a new job. Anxiety about the

impression you make will ensure you make a nervous first impression. Excitement about new challenges will show others your delight in being there. Who do you think your new co-workers would rather work with?

Our attitude is within our control. We can decide if the roller coaster is fun or not. We can decide if this meeting will be boring or not. We can decide if we're going to enjoy our company or not.

Attitude is about understanding what we can and cannot control. When I go to work today, I can decide I'll get a lot done and that it will be a great day. I can also decide it's going to be a horrible day because my coworker Bob is a real drag. When I let Bob define my attitude, I'm giving him control. It doesn't have to be that way. I can't control Bob's attitude; I can only control how I react to him.

Without owning our attitude, we are more likely to be like a chameleon and take on the attitudes of those around us. If we get up and go to work without setting our intentional attitude, we're susceptible to taking on the attitudes of those around us. This naturally happens because we're social. The difference is, if we set an intentional attitude, we get to be the ones influencing those around us.

It's that simple.

What attitudes have you picked up from others showing a boundary problem?

BEVERAGE

Just like we pick a cool beverage on a hot day, the beverage you hold in your hand represents your choices. Think about how you spend your time and money. Think about how hard you try at something new. Think about the investment you put into your friendships and family. We make these choices every day.

We must own our choices! If we don't, like our attitude, we're likely to take on the things those around us ask of us, regardless of whether they're good for us. In this unintentional state, we give our time and spend our money in response to whatever request is made.

An obvious example of the power of unintentional choices is eating. Without a plan or goal for eating, we'll grab whatever is put in front of us. We eat what we see others eat regardless of whether or not we're hungry. We eat the sugary donut because it's in the break room. We overindulge in alcohol because our friends are doing it too.

Many of us have put our minds on autopilot when it comes to our choices. We simply react to what's around us instead of choosing to pursue things that satisfy our deepest desires to be healthy. If we react to everything we see, we'll be like a pinball going this direction and that instead of walking on a path toward our goal.

Our choices are our responsibility, and they are ours to make.

What choices of yours are you leaving up to others?

OBJECT OF BEAUTY

The beautiful object in your imaginary yard represents what *you* value. Is it time with family, your career, or a hobby? It's important to identify what you value because it is something important to protect.

What do you value?

Let's say you value fixing up old cars. You spend time going to classic car shows, searching for parts, and reading car magazines. Your passion is protected by the actions you take. Your time, money, and energy are devoted to what you value and not the things other people value.

We get stuck when we have conflicting values with those around us and expect them to value what we do. Mutual respect is the only way to negotiate how we balance protecting what we value and accepting what others do. It's not all or nothing, as we live and work with people living in their own imaginary, perfect world.

Understanding happens when our conflicting values are seen simply as differences from one yard to the next. We allow each person to protect what they value without making them see things the same as we do

When something is valuable to us, it's our responsibility to protect it. What you value sits in your yard and is under your care. What you value is part of who you are. It's OK to value what others do not. True friends can overlook the differences or, better yet, appreciate them!

Relationships are built around common values, but it's important to acknowledge they will not always line up. Being frustrated that someone else doesn't want to spend time on your hobby is a boundary issue. You are stepping into their yard and dumping your beautiful object there, expecting them to appreciate it like you do.

Protecting your values means saying no to anything that will compromise them. If you value the time you spend on Sunday with your faith community, you'll say no to an early morning tee time or soccer game. If you value your marriage, you will say yes to time spent together. And if you value your health, you will be intentional about caring for it.

What steps will you take to protect what you value?

ATTACHED TO THE FENCE

The thing attached to your fence for the neighbors to enjoy in this visualization exercise represents your gifts. It is an expression of a healthy life sharing itself with the rest of humanity.

Each of us has gifts. We have unique skills and perspectives that allow us to share our gifts with the rest of the world. Too often, however, our gifts have become overgrown with weeds of fear or been shoved in a corner as unimportant. Many people are afraid and stifle the natural urge to be creative. The big losers are all those who could be influenced by the magnificent you.

Scientifically, we know each one of us is unique. No two people have had the exact same feelings, experiences, and gifts. Imagine all people on the earth lined up in neat rows. Then imagine a white bedsheet placed over the top of each head. It would look pretty funny seeing all those "ghosts." Who would want to live in a world where everyone looked the same? Who would want to live in a world where everyone acted the same? Who would want to live in a world where everyone was only a representation of everyone around them?

But, when we hide our unique gifts from others, it's like we're covering ourselves with that white sheet. We might have an ability to cure cancer, make others laugh, or climb mountains—but it won't matter if we hide it.

Strengthening, expanding, honing, and displaying our gifts is up to us. We are the only ones able to practice over and over to get it right. We are the only ones who will have the passion and drive to bring it to fruition. And we are the only ones who can have the courage to share it with the world.

We aren't born with our gifts fully developed. The masters of the world say you will never quit learning about it. When we discover something we thoroughly enjoy, it's a good sign it is a gift. You will have the drive and persistence to pursue it if you love it.

Gifts aren't necessarily performable skills like playing an instrument or painting a picture. Your gift could be meeting new people and getting them to be comfortable, organizing time or ideas, or seeing the deeper meaning of life's unexpected events. Once you identify what it is you do well, you will be able to share it with your neighbors.

What are your gifts?

GATE

The gate represents your ability to manage your thoughts. It has the ability to take what we hear from others and either keep those thoughts out or let them in. It also takes our own thoughts and sends them out or keeps them in. Like one of the stone-faced soldiers guarding Buckingham Palace, you decide which thoughts to let in and which to keep out. You can look each thought up and down and either turn them away or let them in.

We all have continual thoughts going on in our minds. What gives them power is how much we pay attention to them. Mine can jump up and down like popcorn. They're fast and random, changing from second to second. Others build like an orchestra, going from bad to worse. And some are like the beating of a drum that won't stop. It's as if they're in a never-ending loop, constantly attacking with the same repetitive message.

When I realize my thoughts are mine to manage, it is easy to step away from them and see them as separate from myself. "Oh yes," I say, "it's the beating drum again. I'm going to send those thoughts out the gate." Not every thought needs to be believed in or acted upon.

At first, this can be difficult work, but just like riding a bike, soon you are doing it automatically. The gate is your power. Don't leave it open, flopping in the wind.

Our thoughts are our responsibility. Other people may place thoughts in your mind, but once they arrive at your gate, they become yours to manage. Sometimes, like after the leaves have fallen in early autumn, we have cleanup to do. We need to get out the rake, put the leaves in bags, and bring them out to the curb. During a storm, a huge tree limb can fall into your yard, and it needs to be cut up and taken away.

What thoughts do you need to take out to the curb?

Can you see the parallels to life? Let's say someone damages your car. Their insurance may pay for the damages, but you need to take the car in, get an estimate, and get the repairs to be done. If the broken car sits in your yard and you don't take care of it, you're the one without wheels.

After spending years and years wondering if people liked me, I decided one morning it would be good to assume everyone did. This was simply a change in my thoughts. If I believed everyone liked me, I'd give them a more cheerful and positive vibe. It would work especially well if they *didn't* like me. And the best thing was, regardless of how they actually felt about me, I hadn't wasted time fretting they didn't.

But it's not as easy as it sounds. Many of us simply open the gate and leave it open, thinking this is the best way to share our lives. That's all fine and good, but if your yard gets destroyed as people trounce around on it with no limits, no one will want to visit because it will have nothing to offer. If you allow others to mistreat you, steal what you value, negatively affect your attitude, hurt your feelings, alter your choices, and place unhealthy thoughts in your mind, you're not sharing your life but allowing it to be damaged and changed by those around you.

Who is determining the position of your gate?

Picture the gate in your mind. You are the master and can open it whenever you wish or keep it locked so that the thoughts pass by on the outside. The bottom line is that you have the power to choose.

FENCE

The fence represents your boundary. Now that you know what resides in your yard, you'll be able to take responsibility for it. Your fence is the dividing line between your beautifully unique life and the lives of others.

There are a few more ways to care for your yard you'll want to be aware of.

Describe your fence. Picture it in your mind.

BEHAVIORS

Our behaviors are a place we exercise our boundaries, and they carry natural consequences. If we get enough sleep, we're sharp and ready to go the next day. If we manage our money, we have funds saved for an emergency. And if we invest in friendships, we get to both give and receive love. Our behaviors are our responsibility.

On the flip side, if we break the law, we may be fined or locked up. If we overindulge, our bodies will feel the pain, and if we're mean and nasty, friends will be harder to come by. Our behaviors are our responsibility.

What is important when talking about personal boundaries is recognizing what is ours and what is *not* ours. If a friend makes a poor choice and we step in to "take care" of the natural consequences, we do nothing but make sure they'll do it again.

We have a boundary problem.

Just as our skin burns if we put our hand on a hot stove, the natural consequences of bad behavior will teach us not to do it again. When I reduce the sting of a burn by "rescuing" my teenager from a speeding ticket, I take away his ability to learn from it.

Women are particularly prone to being careless with boundaries. We often believe it's our duty to protect our children from any harm well into adulthood. What this does is prevent them from growing up into adults. The lessons will sting and be painful to watch, but the result is better than stepping into your child's yard and taking care of their responsibilities. Parenthood is a time to let go of our children bit by bit so that they're better able to take care of their yard once they leave the nest. They need to have a clear sense of their yard and what they are responsible for.

Allowing people to be responsible for their own stuff is the most loving thing you can do for them. Interrupting their lives because of your boundary issues is the worst thing you can do for both you and them. Allowing others to manage their own lives allows them to gain confidence as they go through difficult times.

This does not mean we don't support and continue to love. It just means we believe in them enough to succeed through their failures and show we are confident in their ability to bounce back. Most of life's lessons involve failing first, figuring out what went wrong, and moving on in a healthier way.

What behaviors show you have a boundary problem?

LIMITS

There is one more principle of boundaries that is extremely important, and it is about limits. By setting limits, we protect our yard and our relationships.

Let's say someone is pounding at your gate, pleading to get in. You ask what is going on. If someone is threatening them with a gun and the only safe place is in your yard, by all means let them in! Tell them the rules so that nothing gets damaged, and allow them a place of rest. If, however, they are pounding on your gate because they're running from the police after breaking the law, the most loving thing to do is to keep the gate closed and not let them in.

What limits would support your boundaries?

Each person has their own unique yard. Each person has their own emotions and attitudes. Each person makes their own choices and finds value in different places and things. Everyone has different thoughts they must manage, predators at their gate, limits to enforce, gifts to share, and love to give and receive. Picturing all the different yards in my neighborhood brings me great joy and allows me to be less judgmental.

All our relationships will be better as we see people in their own yards and not an extension of ours. Having clear personal boundaries is fundamental to strong mental health.

Own Your Life

It's all you. No one else. Blaming keeps you stuck. Unforgiveness keeps you in chains. When you realize your mental health depends on you, you own your life.

In the past, I didn't take responsibility for my mental health. I didn't know I had to. I didn't know how. When I finally discovered cognitive behavior therapy, it was as if a door opened. I walked through, learned the easy strategies to own my own state of mind, and never looked back. It was that simple. I just needed to take responsibility for my feelings, emotions, reactions, and thoughts. If I could do it, you can too.

DIRECTION

The direction of our life is up to us. Owning the direction of our life means we agree and accept this. Our choices, attitudes, friendships, successes, and failures are all within our control. Relying on others for this direction is to place our will under their authority.

Picking up this mantle gives us the proper mindset. Instead of responding to negativity around us, we choose a positive attitude. Instead of waiting for someone else to make the first move of a friendship, we approach others openly. Instead of waiting for someone to discover our talents, we share them in humility.

And instead of blaming others for our failures, we accept responsibility and learn from it. The choice is ours.

It takes courage to own the direction of our life. It is easier to say we didn't have the right opportunities, enough money, or enough time. But courage inspires us to look for and take opportunities. It will never use money as a substitute for determination. And courage will even say no to good things in order to invest in the great.

Owning the direction of our life takes work and intention. Unlike a balloon that floats along with the currents of the wind, we must build a path toward our goals day after day. Small steps each day move us forward. When we accept this principle, the steps aren't laborious but normal.

Brushing my teeth is normal. I don't gripe about doing it every day. My mouth feels clean, and I understand it's important for my physical health. No one else can brush my teeth for me and, frankly, no one else cares if I do it or not. I floss too. I don't wait for the mood to strike me to brush; I take care of it morning and night.

So it goes with our life. There are normal things that must be done to move in the direction we choose. If I want a job as a waiter, I'll find a restaurant, fill out an application, and show my enthusiasm at the interview. If I want a job as a lawyer, I'll go to college, take the LSAT, apply to law schools, finish my course work, and apply for a job. If I want to write a book, I'll write. Pages upon pages. I'll read and research. I'll find an editor and a publisher. I'll show my enthusiasm for what I write to others.

Making decisions about what is normal for our lives starts with where we want to go. When we understand we must own the destination, decisions about what to do become clear. Without the destination in mind, we wander through life and our mind is not free.

What direction is your life going?

When we own the direction of our life, we stop making excuses. When we own the direction of our life, we show courage. When we own the direction of our life, we get unstuck.

WORK ETHIC

Another part of owning our life is determining our work ethic. Our work ethic is decided by how badly we want to get to where we're going. It's a measure of how much we're willing to pay for what we want. It's how much persistence will we show toward what we want.

In her book *Mindset,* Carol Dweck describes the growth mindset and the fixed mindset. Those with a growth mindset have an understanding that their skills can be developed. Those with a fixed mindset believe their skills are fixed and cannot be improved up. It's those with the growth mindset who succeed in life.

In order to work toward something using a strong work ethic, we must first believe the work will accomplish something. It's necessary to have a growth mindset, one open to endless possibilities of the growth which can take place. Without this mindset, we won't spend the energy it takes to get what we want.

Tom Brady was chosen as the NFL's 199th draft choice in 2000. The scouting report on him said he had a poor build, was very skinny and narrow, could get pushed down easily, lacked mobility and the ability to avoid the rush, lacked a strong arm, couldn't drive the ball down the field, and didn't throw a tight spiral. The report ended by calling him a system type player who was not what teams were looking for in physical stature, strength, and mobility.

But what he lacked in natural ability he made up with his strong work ethic. He admits the scouting report was true, and he went to work to become what he is today. Six Super Bowl rings later, he's shown the power of a strong work ethic.

How is your work ethic getting, or not getting, you what you want?

Those with a strong work ethic don't expect others to do things for them. Understanding our personal boundaries strengthens this skill. No knight in shining armor is going to sweep us off our feet and take care of all our needs. A lottery ticket will not solve our financial problems. And our spiritual counselor is not taking care of our soul. But a strong work ethic will allow us to take care of things we are responsible for.

And those of us with a strong work ethic embrace the idea of work. It's how we're wired. We gain satisfaction and energy when we try hard. Whether or not the results come immediately, we are empowered as we put our best effort into all we do.

Our mind is free when we own this part of our life. But a strong work ethic is foundational to pursuing *all* areas of health—physical, mental, and spiritual. Instead of having confusion about wanting things but not putting in the effort we know is necessary, we will be free to pursue all we want out of our life. We will be free to try hard. Free to fail. And free to succeed.

DELAYED GRATIFICATION

Another life skill to grow that will free your mind, allow you to live a healthy life, and get you unstuck is delaying gratification. The process of investing our time, not taking shortcuts, and delaying gratification of the payoff is necessary for a free life.

It takes time to change. During the process, we must delay gratification. Succumbing to our wants, wishes, and whims is often what got us stuck in the first place. Now is the time to delay that gratification and own our life.

Let me tell you how delaying gratification helped me. I was reading the Lord's Prayer and realized something true about myself in the line "and lead us not into temptation, but deliver us from evil."

I discovered my temptation was to judge, and those judgments were putting me in a sad place, full of anguish and grief. Every time I had a negative thought about someone, I sank deeper into the muck of depression. I was gratifying myself with those negative thoughts.

Most of us think gratification—our temptation—has to do with chocolate cake or a shopping spree. The evil we are delivered from is extra pounds or maxing out our credit. But my gratification had to do with the sick part of me that needed to judge others to feel good about myself.

Our gratification can be a destructive behavior. We gratify our need for attention, our desire to be pessimistic, and our fears—the very things that lead us astray. After my realization, every time I would have a negative thought about others, I would repeat over in my mind, "Lead me not into temptation! Lead me not into temptation!" It may have sounded a bit radical if someone could have heard me, but calling myself out on this stopped the madness of gratifying myself by judging others.

What temptation are you gratifying?

Delaying gratification can also be thought of as investing. Instead of splurging on the pretty pink sweater calling my name from the storefront window, I can invest in my financial future by not buying it. Instead of gratifying my lazy nature by binge-watching Netflix, I am investing in my hobby by practicing the piano. Instead of gratifying my desire to look better than others by spending hours getting ready in front of the mirror, I am investing in my spirit by spending time in prayer or meditation. This turns what we may see as denying ourselves into a positive of what we will get.

Delaying gratification doesn't have to happen overnight. We will stumble precisely because the things we were doing *were* gratifying! Be patient with yourself. Find a mantra (like *lead me not into temptation*) or an accountability partner. Talk to yourself about the investment you're making in yourself. Take small steps before you plunge knee-deep into a full-blown radical change. Listen to podcasts. Read a book. See a counselor. Get a coach.

Figure out how to do this. It will change your life.

Take ownership of this part of your life. Delay gratification.

It will free your mind.

RESILIENCE

Another way we own our life is to be resilient.

Have you ever jumped on a trampoline? It's really fun. I get the feeling of flying while I'm in the air, kicking my arms and legs like crazy and laughing like a child. Now, what if you *were* the trampoline? Imagine how it would feel. Some kooky person is giggling and squealing while you take the brunt of their weight. It may not be so fun. But that's life sometimes, and the only way we can make it through in one piece is to snap back into place—just like a trampoline.

The definition of resilience is an object's ability to recoil or spring back into shape after bending, stretching, or being compressed. Just like a trampoline. It also describes a person's ability to recover quickly from difficult conditions.

How resilient are you?

Being resilient when the storms of life hit is necessary to stay unstuck. It's a part of our life we must believe in, develop, and use to have strong mental health. In addition to taking responsibility for the direction of our life, developing a strong work ethic, and delaying gratification, being resilient will free us to succeed and allow us to embrace failure as helpful feedback.

Research shows the primary factor in resilience is having caring and supportive relationships within and outside the family. Anyone who has had the unfortunate opportunity to create a CaringBridge site because of their own or a loved one's illness will tell you the outpouring of support from others is palpable. Knowing others are thinking of them and supporting them on their difficult journey increases their resilience.

Another way to increase our resilience is to not see our problems as insurmountable. This is what got us stuck in the first place. To believe there is always a solution adds strength and creativity when adversity shows up. When we give up on our problems, hyperbolize their extent, or cave under their pressure, resilience flees and we get stuck.

I'll never forget when my pregnant sister-in-law and I were deep in the woods on our cross-country skis. The sun was beginning to go down, and the snow was falling gently on top of a twenty-inch base. Suddenly, her ski binding broke away from her boot and she sank into the snow. We looked at one another in that quiet moment, both knowing there was no possible way to walk back. Forcing ourselves to believe she wasn't going to freeze to death before her baby could be born, we both muttered something about figuring this out.

We shoved away our fear and went into problem-solving

mode. She stared at her broken binding and then had a stroke of genius. She untied the laces from her boot and strung them through the binding before attaching them back to her boot. We made it back. Her baby is now twenty-nine. I'll never forget that moment.

Resilience is also developed when we accept change as a part of life. Having this flexible attitude allows us to be nimble when obstacles present themselves. Think of the trampoline again. If we're inflexible as the hardship hits, we'll take the full force of it and the damage will be great. On the other hand, if we understand things change, we'll accept the predicament, take the hit, and quickly begin the process of bouncing back.

Another way to increase our ability to be resilient is to care for ourselves. We're able to take the brunt of bad news better if we're rested and feel strong. In addition to being connected with others, our ability to have positive self-talk, enforce personal boundaries, and manage our emotions will allow us to recover quickly. We all respond better from a strong body, mind, and spirit than from weak ones.

Resiliency is not a trait people have or don't have. It involves behaviors, thoughts, and actions, which can be learned and developed in anyone. As we become healthier physically, mentally, and spiritually, our resilience naturally becomes healthier too. We have a toolbox of skills and strength to cope with adversity.

BE PROACTIVE

I was out with a friend, Liz, and we ran into my friend Steve. Liz had never met Steve. Through the course of our conversation, we started talking about weddings. Steve's daughter was getting married. Neither Liz nor I had children who were married, and Liz had a video she wanted to show him.

Remember the video that went viral of a wedding party dancing down the aisle instead of walking slowly? It was a hit!

It blew the normal church wedding out of the water, and people loved it.

Liz began looking on her phone for the video. This was quite a while ago, and it was a little tough for even the most tech-savvy. When she finally found it, she asked Steve what his email address was so she could send it to him. (I don't think it was possible at the time to text a video. My oh my, technology has changed.) When Steve gave her his email address, she tried it and the video didn't go through. She tried it again, and it didn't work again. She couldn't get it to go.

I was getting impatient and said, "Liz, I'll give you Steve's email tomorrow." I wanted to move on with our conversation.

She calmly said, "No, that's all right. I'll get it." It took about another thirty seconds, but she finally got it sent.

The next day I was talking to Liz and she asked, "Did you see what I did yesterday?" I immediately knew she was talking about the video, so I apologized for jumping in and telling her what to do. She said, "No, that's okay. But did you see what I did?" I hadn't. She told me, "I had to take care of that video right then because tomorrow I have other stuff to take care of. If I wait until tomorrow, I can't get as much done."

This is being proactive. Not putting off to tomorrow the little snafus of today is the start. Have you ever noticed how often you put something on a list to do later when it could have been done then? It's a bad habit. We either forget to do it later, don't have time to do it later, or don't want to do it later.

Some people suggest that, if a task takes two minutes or less, we should do it as soon as we realize it needs to be done. Instead of looking at the dirty dishes and thinking, "I'll put those in the dishwasher later," just do it.

I've figured out I can unload my dishwasher in less than two minutes. It's easier to stare out the window or peruse the newspaper, but every morning, while my oatmeal cooks, I unload the dishwasher.

And then it's done. Then I'm free to do the rest of the stuff I fiddle around with before I get to work. I don't leave a messy kitchen to see when I get home. If I do, then I have dinner to make *and* dishes to take care of. Things pile up when we aren't proactive.

Successful people don't wait for bad circumstances to show up before they take action to fix something that is almost broken. They buy toilet paper before they run out. They have difficult conversations before emotions blow up and practice gratitude when things are going well.

Our life is less stressful when we are proactive. Instead of keeping a mental list of all the things to take care of tomorrow, we can be present in the moment, make decisions more easily, and be free for spontaneity.

And when life inevitably throws a curveball at us, proactive people have margin in their lives to handle them. They don't have a list of ten things undone along with the regular events of the day *and* a crisis to attend to. It eases the stress of the current situation by not adding on stress from things undone.

For years, I waited to run out of something before I put it on my grocery list. Now I have a backup for the necessities that make life messy when I run out of them. It's not only nice to have backups but also comforting. Instead of sending myself into a panic because I can't run the dishwasher and causing myself to wash the dishes by hand, I calmly go to my backup. It makes my life easy. Life has enough foibles of its own. Why create more?

Being proactive also means not *reacting* to other people's aggressive, negative, or manipulative behavior. Proactivity defines our commitment to a sane mind. It listens and learns. It responds from a place of calm.

When we own the part of our life that is proactive, we take

control of what we can. This is not an attempt to control but to manage what is ours to care for.

What could you do to be proactive today?

Being proactive with our thoughts eliminates unrealistic fears, negative thinking, and blame. It builds up connections with others, positive self-talk, and personal boundaries. Strengthening our mental health to handle life's challenges is proactive.

And being proactive is being responsible for the direction of our lives. It delays gratification for the larger goal. It is courageous and strong. It is ready for the unexpected and also able to handle it when it comes.

Healthy people are proactive in all areas of their life. Owning this part of ourselves will free our mind for more important matters.

SUMMARY

Being mentally healthy will free your mind. When you establish appropriate boundaries, you show great respect for yourself. You're free to be yourself and allow others to do the same. This leads to authenticity, which is freedom. When you manage your thoughts, you're able to navigate the difficulties that come to everyone. When you're connected to others, you fulfill your need to be social. All these help you feel better.

These are the necessary tools to have strong mental health. Connecting with others because we are social beings. Loving yourself as a prerequisite for a healthy mind. Where the two meet and you interact with others, it's necessary to be comfortable with your own personal boundaries in order to have great relationships with others. The final tool is taking ownership of your life by being responsible for its direction, using your work ethic, delaying gratification for your long-term goals, being resilient in difficulties, and being proactive.

Chapter Twelve
FREE YOUR SPIRIT

We all have a spirit. It's the voice in our mind that makes us different from everyone else. It can grow and change. It can be determined, weak, or joyful. It's drawn to like-minded people. It motivates, devastates, or enhances our life.

Our spiritual life is the third leg of the stool. Without it, we tip over and are out of balance. To be healthy, we must step into the spiritual part of ourselves.

Our spirituality has nothing to do with religion, but our religious practice may enhance it. The seven spiritual practices discussed below are essential to getting unstuck. Without them, we're operating at a disadvantage. This is more than a positive mental attitude. This is more than the beliefs we took over from our parents.

Our spirit has nothing to do with our chronological age. It can be an infant, a toddler, a rebellious teen, or a grown-up. Our spiritual age has to do with the lessons we've learned and the perspectives we have. It has nothing to do with our bank account or the number of degrees we hold but is the place that allows us to enjoy life, laugh, and connect deeply with others.

You may not be interested in being a monk, praying to God, or reading Eckhart Tolle. But the truth is, we were all created with a special gift, meant to be shared with humanity. That gift resides in our spirit, the essence of who we are.

I've had many, *many* spiritual questions over my lifetime.

Some have literally lasted for years. Maybe it's because I'm stubborn, or maybe I'm a slow learner. But maybe it's because my spirit will not be satisfied with easy answers or platitudes. The quality of my life depends on the answers.

We get stuck when our spirit is unhealthy, so we must heal from what's ailing it. The only way to heal our spirit is to care for it. As we work to strengthen our spirit, it will heal. Only then will it be free.

This is a game changer.

Faith

There is a scene in *Indiana Jones and the Last Crusade* in which our hero is standing on a ledge with a deep chasm in front of him and a wall on the other side. He needs to get across the abyss, and time is of the essence. It's one of many fascinating spectacles where the audience has no idea how he's going to get out of this one.

He stands at the edge of the wall, where his desperate logic says, "Impossible. Nobody can jump this." It's imperative for him to get to the other side to save his father's life. Indiana begrudgingly recites a clue from the book leading him on this journey. "It's a leap of faith."

The scene cuts to his dying father. As if he can be heard telepathically, he pleads, "You must believe, boy! You must believe!" Indiana Jones puts his hand on his chest, pauses as he looks straight ahead, and takes a big step into the gorge. His foot finds a bridge that was hidden by an optical illusion. The music swells as he follows the almost-invisible bridge to the other side. The audience breathes, and Indiana makes his way to save his father.

I wonder if I will ever have that much faith.

Even though it's just a movie, we have times in our lives where we feel like we're taking a step into a deep gorge. Fear tells us we'll figuratively fall to our death, and the only way across is with faith. We must believe.

Faith is defined as complete trust or confidence in someone or something. Other words used to describe our faith include belief, conviction, reliance, and dependence.

Who or what do you have faith in?

We all have faith. Many people have faith in a spiritual being. Others have faith in science. Some put their faith in an institution, and others have faith in themselves.

It takes faith to have faith. This may sound like a dog chasing its tail. Indiana Jones only had faith in his second step on the bridge because he put his faith behind the first. Faith begets faith. We must begin.

Having faith means we know what we believe in and embrace it. We aren't tossed around by popular opinion. Our beliefs give us something to hold new ideas up to as a way to compare and assess. And when we're confident in what we believe, we no longer have to defend our position but are peaceful about our beliefs.

Let's talk about different areas of faith that help us live a full, effective, and healthy life.

FAITH IN OURSELVES

It's important to have faith in ourselves. Each one of us was given unique gifts to share with the world. Hiding those under a bush serves nothing but our fears. Owning them is a gift to all.

When we have faith in ourselves, we're able to do what we know is right and take a blind step toward a goal, believing it will work out.

Faith in ourselves is not prideful. It's logical. It gives credence to the lessons we've learned along the way. Faith in ourselves listens to the small voice only we can hear. Faith in ourselves ignores negative and hateful comments by others. Faith in ourselves chooses joy over sorrow, hope over despair, gratitude instead of victimization. Faith in ourselves believes in our capacity to show love regardless of whether it comes back to us. Faith in ourselves empowers us to hold up when difficulties arise, believing in our strength to handle them.

FAITH IN OTHERS

Our faith in others is important too because the people in our lives fill in our gaps. We need others to give us a bigger perspective, teach us lessons, and help us along the way. Without faith in others, we are left to our own limited competence.

I have faith in my husband, my friends, and my family. Each one will sometimes disappoint, but overall, they support my life. Without reliance on them, I cannot accomplish as much, feel as fulfilled, or expand my perspective.

We are forced to have faith in many people based on our needs. I have faith in our banker, insurance agent, employees, and neighbors, along with other drivers on the road, airline pilots, judges, and politicians. We put faith in a doctor's opinion when faced with a health crisis and faith in an attorney to draft a will or adoption papers or give advice on selling a business. I have faith in the salesperson's opinion as she sells me clothes and have faith that the cook who prepares my food at a restaurant is doing a good job.

Faith teaches us to trust. This ability is critical to our spiritual health. There are times when we need others to help us through a difficult situation, and we trust them to help us. We desire to share experiences and emotions with others, but first we must trust them to hold confidences and be nonjudgmental with us.

FAITH IN A GREATER POWER

We often find it easy to have faith in others to help us. But faith in something or someone unseen is a different story. Organized religion has disappointed many, and the solution for some has been to do an about-face and walk away.

I remember the first fax I saw. How in the world could someone feed a piece of paper into their machine and have it come out on my end? Did the piece of paper get scrunched up to the size of a phone line and travel through that way? I still don't get it.

How does the weather app on my phone know I just looked at shoes on Zappos on my computer? How does PayPal know how much I pay for my mortgage? How do planes fly? How do they make babies in test tubes? And how can anyone put a swing set together? All of it takes faith.

If all the knowledge of the world were the size of the ocean, I would understand just a thimbleful. It takes faith for me to live in this world. There is more I don't understand than I do.

This is why it's not a big leap for me to go from "Go ahead, you can do the brain surgery, Doctor. I'm not sure what to do, but I have faith in you," to "Go ahead, God, you can guide my life. I'm not sure what to do, but I have faith in you."

MIRACLE

I have a friend, Michelle. She's an ER nurse with scientific training and a strong work ethic. Michelle gets up at four in the morning, drives to our town to swim, puts on her scrubs, and works twelve-hour days.

She's amazing.

A while ago, Michelle told me about her aunt, who is about my age. Her body was ravaged with cancer. Michelle, her aunt, and several relatives had a text-message chain going. They would send each other prayers for the aunt's healing each day.

The cancer was really bad, and the text-prayers seemed like a lost cause.

But in December I got this text from Michelle: "I can't even believe it. My aunt sent a text this morning . . . she saw Jesus during the PET scan in Rochester . . . he touched her and healed the cancer in her lung and then touched her liver and healed the tumors there . . . she wondered if it was her imagination, but no cancer is left. Doctors over there were so amazed!!! Praise God who is and always was!!!"

This was two years ago. I get chills reading the text again. You can believe what you want, but I choose to believe this was a miracle. There is something out there much, much bigger than me. It seems arrogant and stubborn to hold on to the notion that things are defined by my ability to understand them.

I'm smart enough to know I don't know everything. This is where my faith in God takes over.

FAITH-BASED COMMUNITIES

The Blue Zones by Dan Buettner describes the research done in places around the world where people live longer than anywhere else. Their research has shown that people who are part of a faith-based community tend to have good ways to relieve stress, support positive behaviors, and have purpose for their lives. In addition, they put their family first, eat healthier, and move more naturally. No faith-based community is perfect, just as none of us are perfect. But the research shows that those involved in a faith-based community live longer.

Another reason it's good to have faith in someone or something beyond yourself is that it increases your perspective. Left to ourselves, we will come up with "the Bible according to me." Although it's an easy book to read, it will be self-centered and limited in perspective. Faith only in ourselves is like a stagnant pond with no inflow of fresh water.

BUT FAITH WAS NOT ENOUGH

I've always been religious. As a child, our family faithfully went to church each Sunday. On Easter, my mom would sew special outfits for my sisters and me because it was the holiest day of the year. I learned to go to confession. After college, I joined a Bible study and then joined a church. My husband and I met there and are on the same page as to how we practice our faith.

But it wasn't enough when I was stuck.

Faith in God is like staring at a gorgeous painting, captivated by all it has to offer. Faith is believing it is the most magnificent painting in all the world. Faith is not needing any other painting to satisfy your desire for beauty. Faith is commitment to the painting.

But faith is a one-way street. It is complete trust or confidence in someone or something. When I was depressed, all the faith in the world would not relieve my pain. I could pray and love God, but faith alone was not solving my problem.

Healing from depression required action along with my faith. I had to pursue my physical and mental health and accept I was valuable to God. I needed to take action and participate in my healing. Faith requires us to act as if it's going to work.

My faith in God didn't force me to practice gratitude, so I stayed depressed. I believed that I would have life after death, but this hope wasn't helping my sorrow in the moment. Although I knew God is love, I didn't feel it from either myself or others. My faith in God added meaning to my life, but it was still endlessly difficult. My faith in God did not expose my life's purpose because my depression was like a wet blanket over my life.

To do something with our faith, we need to take these spiritual actions: practice gratitude, hold onto hope, learn to love both ourselves and others, choose joy, find meaning, and fulfill our purpose. These help us live a healthy life. These aren't just fluffy words for churchgoers; they are practical steps for all of us.

Faith is our ability to see that life is more than the sum of our own actions but also mysterious and wonderful. Faith is believing without seeing. It takes courage to have faith. It takes faith to have faith. Our spiritual self requires faith. To ignore it is to hold ourselves back from our own spiritual maturity. Without faith, we'll get and stay stuck.

WE ALL HAVE FAITH IN SOMETHING

Knowing what we have faith in will determine our actions. If I feel stuck in a bad job, knowing what I have faith in will help with the next step. If I have faith in myself, I will look for a new position, confident I'll be able to make a good choice. If I have faith in my employer, I will voice my concerns and wait for them to make changes. If I have faith in God, I will pray and seek guidance. I may also have faith in all these and take several steps at once.

If I don't understand what or who I have faith in, I'll get stuck by *waiting* for something to happen. If I don't acknowledge my own abilities, I won't look for a new job. If I don't have faith in my employer, I could be frustrated and think negatively about my position. And if I don't have faith in God, I will be left to deal with the trouble on my own.

Faith is a muscle, just like the rest of these spiritual principles. If we haven't exercised it, it will be weak. The problem is, faith is hardest to come by when we need it most. Death, divorce, job loss, sickness—these are times when we need to rely on who or what we have confidence in. It's difficult to build faith in yourself in the middle of a divorce. It's hard to have confidence in God after a tragedy if you don't already know Him. And it's hard to have faith in the company that just laid you off because they were downsizing.

FAITH DETERMINES OUR ACTIONS

Every professional athlete is confident in their ability to do their sport. Without this confidence, they would not be a pro. Faith is our confidence for life. It's trust that, whatever life throws at us, we'll be able to keep playing the game like a pro. It empowers us to go the extra mile and be resilient in the face of difficulty.

It happens to all of us. Events enter our life and shift its whole trajectory. Without warning, we're forced to deal with the fallout. We feel like we're on a carnival ride, which makes us sick to our stomach. We scream to get off, but it's not possible. There's no end. No off switch.

If your child is in a life-threatening accident, faith will determine your actions. Faith in yourself will cause you to ask questions and help guide the course of treatment. Faith in the hospital will allow you to trust their recommended course of care. Faith in God will bring you to your knees, asking for guidance and peace. The faith and trust in any of these will empower you to take the right action.

In Laura Hillenbrand's book *Unbroken*, a WWII soldier is captured and tortured unmercifully by the Japanese. After enduring years of this, he is finally freed at the end of the war. He credits his newfound faith in God with the strength to forgive his captors and not suffer any longer in his life. Faith is empowering beyond what many of us can imagine.

Faith is a critical spiritual component of our lives.

Faith determines our actions. The depth of our faith causes us to either freak out or calmly take the next step. It makes us feel out of control or eerily peaceful despite tragedy. It can lead us anywhere on a spectrum of actions from militancy to surrender. Who or what we have faith in directs our steps, our emotions, and the direction of our life.

GRATITUDE

Just be grateful for what you have! We may have heard others deliver that line when we complained that we did not have what our friends had, that our circumstances were looking dire, or that a relationship was going bad. Just being told to be grateful, however, doesn't work.

It needs to be a strategy for your life.

Have you known people who are grateful for almost everything? Do you suspect they're faking it? Yeah, I did too, and it made me angry. "They're wearing rose-colored glasses," I argued. "No one can be grateful in *that* situation."

What I really meant was, *I* could not be grateful in that situation. Or, more precisely, I *would not* be grateful.

"Why be grateful?" I asked myself. "How does it benefit me? Why should I practice it? And why is it so darn hard to do?"

As we practice gratitude, the negative thoughts melt away, our heart becomes lighter, our mood becomes more desirable, and our smile shows up and elicits smiles from others. Forget the whitening toothpaste and makeup—a happy heart and smile will make us more beautiful than ever.

HOW DOES IT BENEFIT ME?

Which is easier to carry in your mind: "I have a good job, good kids, and a good husband" or "I have a crappy job, uncooperative kids, and a loser husband"? The truth doesn't even matter. It's what you tell yourself the truth is.

Being grateful is an easier way to live. The first thought allows you to move on. The second thought is like wearing a backpack filled with concrete. It's heavy and irritates you all day.

It takes effort and creativity to be grateful, but after the effort, you will feel lighter and less burdened. In the long run, you will have a happier and more fruitful life.

Who would you rather be around: a person who complains about the weather, or a person who talks about how grateful they are to be alive? Would you rather spend the afternoon with someone who sees the best in people or someone who is grumpy because their friend said something nasty to them? Who would you ask to help solve a problem: someone who describes how grateful they are that their latest struggle, like yours, taught them some valuable lessons—or someone who will bring up all the bad things that happened to them when they had a similar problem?

When we're grateful, more people will want to be around us.

WHY PRACTICE IT?

We look better when we're grateful. It's impossible to be angry and grateful at the same time. The energy we feel when we're grateful is peaceful as opposed to the tense energy we feel when we're angry. Anger is exhausting and ugly. Gratefulness is refreshing and beautiful. How would you rather look?

Whatever we focus on grows. When gratitude becomes a habit, we will no longer need to exert so much energy to come up with an inventive way to see the positive. The reasons to be grateful will be easy to see. As we freely shift our focus to gratefulness, we feel less stress.

Being grateful gives us a leg up on the competition. When we focus on the positives in a situation, we learn to act from a strong position. Instead of fear driving our decisions, we are in a capable, calm, and clear frame of mind. This is where our best work is done. Instead of focusing on what is wrong, we can see what is right with a situation and take the next step.

When we're grateful, positive words come from our mouths. Those who hear us will be drinking honey, not vinegar. Not only will they enjoy it more, but we will too. Those positive words and emotions create strength in our body and peace in our mind.

It's also easier to be resilient when we're grateful for the opportunity in front of us. Instead of taking on the burdens of each setback, we focus on the positives coming from them and forge ahead. Burdens are difficult to carry. Optimism is lighter. In the midst of difficulty, when resilience is needed to move ahead, gratefulness is a much easier path.

When I was depressed, I was not grateful. The obvious blessings were covered in sadness and despair. I looked at what I didn't have instead of what I did. Not only did this weaken me mentally, but it was physically exhausting too. Instead of being grateful, I was hopeless. I wasn't a bad person; I just didn't have the tools. I didn't understand the power of these spiritual principles to free my spirit.

Learning to change our thinking toward gratitude is a good strategy to be healthy. It reduces the strain or anxiety we have for being stuck and provides energy to discover a way out.

FOCUS ON THE GOOD

My dad recently passed away. When he was in failing health and was reduced to just a shadow of the man he used to be, sad emotions came without warning, reducing me to tears. The last time it came upon me, it took quite a while to even speak. The emotions were that raw. I began to talk about his loss of dignity and how horrified he would be if he knew what his body was doing to him.

Then I asked myself what I expected in this situation. He was ninety-one years old. Did I think he would live forever? What did I want for him? Why was I so sad? What could I do about it?

So many of my thoughts led to a dead end. There was nothing I could do about my dad's suffering. He was dying and it was just plain sad. My mom, too, was caught in the grips of dementia on her way toward the end of life. They wasted away day after day in confusion.

But other thoughts lifted my heart. We had eighty-nine good years with Dad before dementia took over. He had been a wonderful father, and I was grateful for all he did, all he taught me, and how he purely loved me. I was grateful my parents could be together in a memory care unit. He lived in a comfortable, loving environment with capable and amazing caregivers. Almost all my life, things had been rosy with my parents. When my focus changed, peace came over me.

What we focus on is our choice. Do we focus on the disputes we're having with friends or the fact that we can get up every day, be gainfully employed, and see the sunshine? Do we focus on our nagging knee pain or how tasty a peach is, the fact our cars take us wherever we want to go, and the beauty of snow?

We can teach our minds to go to positive, content, and peaceful places. It has to do with focus and intention. Gratitude is like a windshield wiper that wipes away the raindrops so we can clearly see the road ahead. Gratitude will change our attitude for the better and help us be healthy.

What are you grateful for today?

HOPE

Just like all spiritual practices, hope is a choice. It's simply a decision made in our minds to view the future as good. Hope allows us to believe we can get unstuck from any puddle we're in.

We can choose not to be hopeful in order to avoid disappointment. If we hope for nothing, we will never be disappointed. But being hopeless is a sad way to live. The weight of living without hope is greater than the weight of some disappointment. We get to decide which we'll carry.

We sometimes say we've "lost" hope. This happens because of failures, time without results, and people who speak defeat into our life. Hope brings joy. If we hold onto hope, we live with joy in the moment. If we lose it, set it down, or throw it into the river, we live without joy.

Nothing has ever been accomplished without someone first hoping it can be done. Hope generates ideas, motivates people to act, and keeps us going when inevitable failures arrive. Hope is our rocket fuel. It propels us forward despite the obstacles we see or fear. Hope is necessary to climb over the challenges of life. Hope is a brand-new day with opportunities waiting to be discovered. Hope is a lifeline. Hope is your own. Hope is a choice.

People may say you're crazy to be hopeful. Be careful to weigh other people's opinions before you take them on as your own. When we take on other people's lack of hope as our own, we're weighed down by their disappointments and fears. It has an equally negative impact.

Why not hope? Keeping your heart and mind open to all the good that can happen will cause you to be aware of it when it comes across your path.

TEETER-TOTTER

We can think of skepticism as synonymous with being careful. From that point of view, hope equals carelessness. We would all rather be careful than careless.

How, then, can I be hopeful? Think of a teeter-totter. On the one side, you have hope and carelessness. On the other, skepticism and carefulness. Which side do you want to ride?

Thankfully, life is not all or nothing, this or that, black or white. Like on a teeter-totter, there are all kinds of places in between. But still, we must choose a side to sit on. The danger of being hopeful and careless is that we get hurt. The danger of being skeptical and careful is that we miss opportunities.

To me, it's better to run the risk of being hurt than to miss out on opportunities. Of course we shouldn't jump into a stranger's car in a dark alley in the middle of the night, hopeful they will get us safely home. We should, however, take a ride from an Uber driver if it's pouring rain, hopeful they can get us home.

When we sit on the side of hope, we see opportunities. These are treasures that come into our life without us necessarily asking for them. It's a mindset that looks for the good, reasonably assesses danger, and gets us out of the mud puddle that has us stuck.

PRACTICE HOPE

Our ability to hope can come from the experience of all things working out in our life. A stronger hope muscle is developed when things have gotten difficult and we have not caved in to the pending gloom. Exercising hope builds more hope. Each time we *choose* to think on the positive, healthy, energetic, hopeful next steps, we grow the muscle that can help us during difficult times.

Why not hope? Why not believe all things will work out for our benefit? None of us knows what the future holds. The more life we experience, the more we can take note of the crazy, unexpected, or random things that happen for our benefit. Even if things go terribly wrong, we have not spent the time leading up to the disaster in a negative, pessimistic place.

Being hopeful is a conscious effort on our part. We have to work to take whatever is in front of us and paint a silver lining around it. Having a full stomach and being well rested also help. Hanging around others who are hopeful is another way to stay in the "hope zone."

Being hopeful frees our spirit. It's both a vulnerable and courageous place. Being hopeful is strong and attractive. It's playful yet serious. Hope is magical and the secret to success. It's a necessary characteristic to achieve big things. Hope is the antidote to fear. It isn't a strategy but a critical component for a great life.

Practice hopefulness.

What will you hope for today?

JOY

Joy is better than sorrow. Happy is better than sad. Cheer is better than gloom.

Joy is a combination of contentment and freedom.

Wouldn't it be amazing to feel that all the time?

You can. Joy does not depend on your circumstances. Joy is a choice, and sometimes we need to dig deep for it. It's always available and will be more readily accessible when we have a storage room full of it in our hearts.

Every day we can find things not to be joyful about. The traffic, our jobs, the economy, wars. There are also things we can be joyful about every day. The breath in our lungs, relationships, flowers, the sun. Which ones will you choose to focus on?

Joy is internal. It's like the blood flowing through our veins. It's life-giving, and everyone has it. It builds muscle. We can get it from others to save our lives. It heals. It will keep us alive and healthy.

Joy is an emotion we must choose. When reacting to the events in our lives, joy can determine our next move if we let it. A friend of mine got a flat tire on a dreadfully hot day. She was grateful she had AAA and gave them a call. It turned out many cars were stalling that day because of the intense heat, so she had to wait for several hours for a tow.

She chose to be joyful. Instead of stewing in the heat and inconvenience, she had a lovely conversation with a gentleman nearby and used the time to reflect on her blessings. Soon the truck came.

What would you do in a similar situation?

Joy is a state of mind. It's a place of contentment, resolve, happiness, and peace. Joy is contagious and makes you more attractive to be around. It doesn't have to be bubbly. It flows through your veins and will sustain your spiritual life. Practicing joy will allow you to see any situation in a bright light. Joy makes any situation better.

Joy is a choice, but it's also a muscle. If joy is your goal, it's time to hit the gym and build it. It will take hard work and repetition. You'll have to push beyond what's comfortable and sweat like crazy. Gratitude will be your foundation. These are the weights you'll have to keep lifting to build joy.

Practice joy.

MEANING

Meaning is the message we get from the events in our life. Seeing meaning in the circumstances of our everyday lives is a spiritual practice. It can make sense of the situation when things don't go well, understanding the events in our lives as a wonderful journey in which each previous event adds to the next.

Recently, I got a text message that brought me to happy and grateful tears. It was tremendously meaningful to me. The message I received told me that something I did mattered to the other person. The message was genuine and vulnerable. This is what life is about.

Meaning in our lives can be obvious, but much of it has to be looked for. In high school, I dated a really cute guy who was a bit of a rebel. It wasn't long before he fell for another, and I

So Now What?

was heartbroken. Later, I realized the other woman did me a favor. Without her interference, I could have gone down a path not right for me.

In college, I dated a really great guy, but we weren't meant for each other. By my senior year, it was obvious to both of us, and we parted ways. Later in my life, I realized dating him through college kept me out of a lot of trouble, and I'm grateful for it.

After college, I dated someone completely different than me. The moment I said yes to the first date, I knew it wasn't the best. It took quite a while, however, for my heart to catch up with my head. Eventually we broke up, but I learned valuable lessons along the way.

And finally, I met my husband. He was rebellious (in a good way), had different experiences, was a really great guy, and saw life differently than me. We fell in love. Many years later, I realized how meaningful this series of events was. I was looking for something, but none of the first three fit the bill. I was still growing up myself and couldn't quite settle. I'm grateful for the sorrowful but meaningful experiences. Without them, I would not be who I am today.

We can find meaning even in our failures. You may have had a string of frogs before you found your prince too. Have you ever considered how each one was meaningful and pointed you to the place you are today? It's not always obvious in the midst of it, but the seemingly random circumstances of our lives can have profound meaning.

Meaning is important because it's how we grow and develop. Without reflecting on what just happened, we're prone to make the same mistakes or stay in unhealthy life patterns.

Parenthood has been a marvelous experience for me. Each step along the way, I've learned new things. The bigger meaning, to me, is what I've learned about God. In my system of beliefs, God is my parent and I am His child. As I've looked at my children over the years, I have reflected on how God sees me and how I see Him. It has expanded my perception and faith. To me, it's a great illustration of how much love He has for us and how we can also frustrate Him to no end.

Finding meaning can also free us from sorrow. The mistakes I've made over my life, although difficult, are freeing when I find meaning in them and understand the lessons they revealed. After many years attending our church, my husband and I left because of some misunderstandings. We assumed some things, and they did too. We felt rejected and left to find another faith community.

It was a lonely time. Faith is at the core of my being. Being around like-minded individuals once a week feeds my soul. Although trying new congregations was good and we met many fantastic people and heard great messages, it was still sad because of the friends we had left.

Eventually we returned to our original congregation. I will never completely understand the path that led us there, but I have found meaning in the steps of the journey. Finding the meaning has freed me from the sorrow I had experienced. I am grateful for it and am glad it all unfolded the way it did.

COINCIDENCE?

It was 2002. A new friend was into scrapbooking, and I went to a "party" to find out all about it. I was mesmerized by this concept. Scrapbookers takes photos, organize them, and put them into pretty books with stickers and colorful shapes.

Let me tell you, I consider myself fairly crafty, but there are tons of other things I would rather do with my time than art projects. This scrapbooking thing, however, had me hook, line, and sinker. I bought a bag full of stickers and scissors. There seemed to be an endless supply of gadgets and paper to buy. No one would ever call me impulsive, but I dove right off the deep end with this new hobby.

My niece was graduating from high school that year. I didn't know her at all because of a nasty divorce and the distance between us, but I wanted to do something for her. My scrapbooking friend suggested I put together a book with pictures of all the cousins this niece did not know.

I got so excited I could hardly stand it! I shot off emails to all my siblings, asking them to get me pictures of them and their children. We planned a date to get all the kids together to do a group photo for their long-lost cousin. Each family got several pages, and I added narrative to describe who we each were and what we enjoyed. The book was put together in no time with lots of love between the pages.

My parents attended the graduation and delivered the scrapbook. It opened a whole new chapter for my niece. She didn't know she had all those cousins, aunts, and uncles in Minnesota who loved her dearly. Now she had pictures to prove it.

Miracles began to occur after the graduation. Her parents' marriage reconciled after fifteen years. I lost my interest in scrapbooking, and my new friend moved away.

Coincidence? I don't think so.

Meaning is not always easy to find, but finding meaning in your circumstances will give you a fuller and richer life.

What has been meaningful to you today?

PURPOSE

We all have a purpose. To know what it is, step into it, and go after it with gusto is the best way to live. Many of us chase after someone else's purpose or our perceived notion of what other people think our purpose should be. Some are afraid of their purpose or don't believe they have one.

But it's there. We just need to find it.

Finding our purpose can be simple. Think about the things you do that feel good deep down in your soul. They aren't necessarily easy or without trepidation, but you're in the zone when you're doing them. Time goes quickly. Motivation isn't a problem. You love to talk about it, read about it, and learn more about it.

We could also ask, what is it that we are willing to sacrifice for? What will we spend our time doing regardless of the cost involved? When we find it, we'll know our purpose.

We'll feel like we've got more than we gave when we offer our purpose to the world. We are made to give but, most often, we want to get. The easiest way to get is to give. It's counterintuitive but true. Giving is fulfilling. Regardless of what it costs, we will understand deep inside we are doing exactly the right thing both for ourselves and others.

The life of a teacher shows us the power and influence purpose can have. We each probably remember a teacher or two who had a tremendous impact on our lives. When teachers are doing what they were created to do, they can change a child's life for the better. In the midst of chaotic classrooms and routine, their words and actions transform lives. A student embraces a new idea, gains confidence as they master a subject, or find their own purpose in the process of learning.

Purpose is an internal push that is almost too powerful to resist. If a child were running toward a moving car, you would rush to rescue the child from being hit. It's the same with our purpose. When we feel the passion, we move into action. We don't overthink things, stall for weeks at a time, and come up with a list of excuses. We simply act.

Our purpose is in our soul and wants to show itself. Just follow its lead. It's more than an impulse. It's a drive. It's not filled with excitement but pursuit. It won't leave us alone until we acknowledge it.

Finally, purpose gives us satisfaction. When we are doing what we were created to do, we are satisfied. Each one of us has a different fire in our belly that will quench the thirst we have for meaning. Go ahead and live that way!

Our purpose will never burn bridges or cause destruction in our life. It will only build on what we have. It won't call us to leave our spouse, ignore our previous experiences, or run for the hills. Each part of our life is a piece of what we are meant to be.

Rick Warren, author of the book *The Purpose Driven Life*, says, "If you want to find your purpose in life, find your wound." That was absolutely true for me. The wounds left by the years of anxiety and depression became my purpose to inspire others to live a healthy life. They were not wasted years. I don't regret any of the steps along the way. I believe they were necessary to bring about the work I do today. Purpose brings freedom.

DEPRESSION

We also have unique stories. Mine is depression. It took a long time to finally eradicate it from my life. It's my purpose to tell others my story so they won't have to suffer like I did. It's my purpose to talk about depression because there's so much misunderstanding. Both those who suffer and those who don't can benefit from hearing my story.

This isn't about me. It's about the story. It's about depression, which strikes so many of us. It's about helping others with the same struggle. It's about healing.

It's about the common good.

My purpose also comes from my biggest weaknesses. My inability to cope emotionally with life, care for my body, and see myself as worthwhile is where my strength comes from. The story was created out of my struggle. The growth came from the lessons I learned. The beauty can be seen in my healing. I understand the pain and difficulty.

Our culture has difficulty discussing and understanding depression. As someone who walked this path for decades, I understand its twists and turns. I've been on the inside and have a message both for those who suffer and those who don't. I was given the trial to shed light on it.

What's your talent? What's your story? Who could benefit from them? Who could get unstuck because of what you have to offer?

LIFE'S A SNOWBALL

One thing leads to another. Our lives are not simply a series of random events but a series of events that build on one another like a snowball rolling down a hill. It gets bigger and stronger with each turn. It can be revealing your purpose.

The older we get, the easier this is to see. Consider these seemingly random events that have brought me to where I am today.

I love to play Monopoly, so I make a worksheet to make it easier.

Because of my organizational skills, my dad suggests I go into accounting.

My employer at the accounting firm has me give a presentation and I realize I'm comfortable with public speaking.

My employer has me attend association meetings where I meet a man who tells me about a position at his company.

I take a new position at a very large company.

The big company hires me as an independent contractor.

My husband and I start a business (which I've already done as an independent contractor).

So Now What?

We purchase two buildings and charge rent (just like Monopoly).

I become a public speaker (a skill I enjoyed early in my career).

. . . all because I enjoyed playing Monopoly and went into accounting.

Here's another string:

I decide to go to a women's conference (on my own nickel).

I hear a speaker who I really enjoy.

We begin emailing back and forth because we are both doing something new in our life.

I hire her as my coach (and I'm not a big spender).

She helps me discover my love of writing.

I start a blog.

. . . all because I went to the women's conference.

And another:

My neighbor decides to participate in the inaugural Mankato Marathon even though he's never been a runner.

I am so proud of him and want to be involved, so I volunteer.

During the race, I see so many different kinds of people, and I decide to run a half marathon.

Crossing the finish line leaves me more empowered than ever in my life.

I take the crazy step of signing up for a full marathon.

My training partner becomes a great friend and leads me to a wonderful church with amazing people.

I qualify for and run the Boston Marathon.

. . . all because my neighbor decided to do something he'd never

done before.

The funny twist to this story is my neighbor didn't even participate that first year because he had a blood clot form just weeks before the event. Regardless, it changed the trajectory of my life!

Life is a snowball. Each experience builds on the previous ones. It's not always evident right away and is rarely linear. When we look back on it, however, it's amazing and ironic. The steps in our lives reveal how we are living our purpose.

Pay attention to the events that leave you with a lasting impression. Those are the clues to what fulfilling your purpose is about. The events may be happy, painful, or exhilarating. Most importantly, they have an impact on you that doesn't go away.

Recognize the process. It will help you keep your eyes open for the next opportunity. Be open to new experiences, even if they aren't exactly in your plan right now. It's incredible when you open yourself up what will come your way and be the next step in your journey.

Finding your purpose will keep you moving forward. Purpose is a driver, a mover, and a motivator. Living your purpose is a spiritual practice.

List a series of events that brought you to where you are today. What are those events telling you about your purpose?

LOVE

Books and books have been written about love. Poems and songs. Plays and movies. It is the root of most of both our happiness and heartache. Love is critical to our well-being. It's in our DNA. Without it, we can't be healthy.

And it's the key to getting unstuck.

Loving ourselves and others is the solution to all our problems. It's the key to our happiness. Love is the basic element needed to be productive, help others, and live in peace. Without love, we wander through our lives without direction or meaning. And yet it's so elusive.

Love is both concrete and mysterious. It's necessary yet easy to ignore. It's difficult to understand and can be difficult to accept. There are many different kinds of love. Sometimes it must be tough and other times very tender.

We all need love. Even your curmudgeonly neighbor needs it. Your rebellious teenager needs it. The successful businessman needs it. You need it. The more we understand our need to both receive and give love, the healthier we will be.

Our ability to love both ourselves and others is important. Leave either of those out and our love is lopsided. It's a balancing act, but the first step on the tightrope has to be loving ourselves. Without that, we will only be able to love others in counterfeit ways.

My basic question as I walk through life is, "How do I love you?" I love my husband differently than I love my child. I love my friends differently than I love my coworkers. And I love people I don't know differently than my acquaintances.

The times we get stuck in our lives are simply pointing out that we need to learn more about love. We're lacking in our love either for ourselves or for others.

TRAINING

When I train for a marathon, I prepare for eighteen weeks. Along with putting in many miles, I make sure I sleep enough, eat the right foods, and do yoga to keep my muscles stretched out. But all that is not enough. I must also keep a positive mind-set, discipline myself to follow the training schedule, and organize my social life so it doesn't interfere. And even those things aren't enough. I need to register for the event, buy the right gear, and understand the weather may dole out a challenge I didn't anticipate. And this is all about just running a silly marathon. What about love?

To love completely, I must be prepared. When my body, mind, and spirit are at their best, they are prepared for love. But that's not enough. I have to stay positive about people, discipline myself not to judge and compare, and give others my time if that is what's required. Even doing these things is not enough. I need to think about how to love each person best, be reflective about what it means to love, and avoid quick reactions to people. Love demands we focus on the other person instead of ourselves. It also requires us to love ourselves so that we're not damaged and unable to give more.

We must train well in order to love. We must be healthy and prepared to do it well. And even then, we'll need to deal with things we can't anticipate. If we want to love at our best, we need to be at our best.

A WELL-THOUGHT-OUT DEFINITION

To quote the Bible: Love is patient, love is kind and is not jealous; love does not brag and is not arrogant, does not act unbecomingly; it does not seek its own, is not provoked, does not take into account a wrong suffered, does not rejoice in unrighteousness, but rejoices with the truth; bears all things, believes all things, hopes all things, endures all things. Love never fails.

This is a definition of perfect love summed up in a way that has stood the test of time. Love is all these amazing things.

But what if *we're* not? What if we're neither patient nor kind? What if we're jealous and arrogant? What if we have a nasty streak where we brag, are selfish, and are easily drawn into drama? What if we constantly keep score? What if we don't care about the truth as much as we care about our feelings? What if we're sick and tired of believing the best, holding onto hope, and hanging in there? What if we fail?

All of us fail at love sometimes. And when we try to force ourselves back into the perfect definition of love, it's like trying to put on a pair of jeans that are too tight. They don't fit and we're uncomfortable, *but we're going to love, damn it!*

This doesn't work. We can't fake it till we make it. Those jeans simply don't fit, and we have to put on the bigger size where there is more grace for our imperfections and weaknesses. We have to wear jeans that don't cut off our circulation.

COMING FROM THE RIGHT PLACE

If we're loving out of obligation or fear, it's like wearing a pair of skinny jeans that have no give. It hurts and we easily grow tired. We can hardly wait to take those stinkin' jeans off and put on yoga pants.

We can think that loving others means jumping at every opportunity to help. But if it leaves us exhausted, we're not loving at all. We're stepping into a situation to feel needed. Our desire to help comes from a place of need within ourselves, not from a cheerful heart. If our actions don't come from a loving heart, it's better not to help at all.

When we love from the love we feel for ourselves, it's easy. We give time or money because love has far more value. Patience comes easily as we seek another's benefit. We can be kind in the face of anger because our love for the other comes from a deep love of ourselves. Love doesn't need to brag or be arrogant because we are secure. This kind of love stays hopeful in the light of difficulties as a way to bring reconciliation about. But it can't be forced. We can only love others to the extent we love ourselves.

ART

In *The Art of Loving*, Erich Fromm describes love as an art form. Like any artist attempting to perfect their craft, love must be practiced. We must master the theory of love and master the practice of love.

And it starts with self. To Fromm, "the love for my own self is inseparably connected with love of any other being." He describes this paradox as unavoidable.

How do we resolve the dichotomy? How is it possible to love both ourselves and others at the same time? To combine the two seems impossible to some and sinful to others. We fear selfishness if we step into the pool of self-love yet are weak if we step into the pool of love for others and are unable to swim.

If I go into brain surgery, I want Dr. Surgeon to be well rested, capably assisted, and experienced. Let's say Dr. Surgeon's friend Bob asks for help moving a few things the night before my surgery. If Dr. Surgeon subscribes to the idea that his friend's requests should always come before his own, he will happily help. The things Bob and Dr. Surgeon move are heavy, and Dr. Surgeon strains his back.

The next day, during my brain surgery, Dr. Surgeon is a little foggy as he deals with his back strain. Although he is able to perform the surgery fairly well, the twinge in his back causes him to make a slight error and I end up paralyzed for life. This would be tragic.

If Dr. Surgeon believes that self-love is a prerequisite for loving others, he will ask Bob what needs moving. Finding out the items are heavy, Dr. Surgeon will confess to Bob the risk of not being fresh the next morning for surgery could have disastrous consequences. Dr. Surgeon understands his limitations. He may brainstorm with Bob to find someone else to help.

This is an extreme example. Hopefully brain surgeons aren't hauling pianos for their friends late into the night before they operate. Most reasonable people have an idea of their limitations and the risks involved. But this example may still apply to you.

To me, love of self and others means love is a circle where we are both giving and receiving love simultaneously. When the circle is broken by our inability to either give or receive, we're unable to love fully. Likewise, the better we are at both giving and receiving, the stronger our circle becomes.

How are you practicing the art of love?

LOVE IS NATURAL

According to Dr. Caroline Leaf, a cognitive neuroscientist with a PhD in communication pathology, we are wired for love. And I believe it! When we act in a loving way, we feel content and free. When we act out of negative thoughts and emotions, we will be anxious and tense.

We are in our natural state when we are loving. Seeing the glass as half full is natural for us. We were created to be peaceful, keep a clear mind, and offer charity. This is natural, fulfilling, and possible.

Our human survival depends on love. In Charles Darwin's book *The Descent of Man and Selection in Relation to Sex*, he mentions the word "love" eighty times, the word "sympathy" fifty-two times, and the words "survival of the fittest" just three times. He did not place his emphasis on the survival of the fittest, as we have often heard, but on mutual aid and love for each other as the key to human success both as individuals and as a species.

SELF

When we care for our body, mind, and spirit, we're able to go out into the world and show powerful and authentic love. We'll be able to give more, share more, and encourage more. Without this self-love, those around us get a weak and ailing love.

Let's say you've been unable to get a good night's sleep over the past week, which has you exhausted. Work has been stressful, and you haven't been eating right. You just had a fight with your spouse when the phone rings. You answer it out of obligation, and a friend asks if you can help at a spaghetti dinner fundraiser Friday night. He pleads with you because he's tried so many people but they're all busy.

You don't have plans on Friday. The spaghetti dinner is raising money for a good cause. What do you say? Many people would automatically say yes. The cause is good, their friend needs help, and their spouse can wait.

Do you feel like you have to volunteer because no one else will? Are you afraid the friend will feel rejected if you say no to his request? Are you using this as an excuse to avoid the difficult conversation with your spouse? Do you feel guilt over how little you give to the needy?

None of these are good reasons to say yes or no. The only good place to give from is a joyful heart. Giving out of obligation, fear, shame, or guilt is not giving at all. All that does is feed those negative emotions, which are fraudulent displays of love.

To not love yourself is to not love others. Like the surgeon who needs to get plenty of sleep to perform well, we need to take care of ourselves too. The way to solve this dichotomy is to not react to other's requests out of false motives but to love cheerfully. When we're strong, confident, and grateful, not only are we *able* to give to others, but we *want* to.

How to Love

Now that we're clear about loving ourselves, our question is how and why to love others. The answers may surprise you.

When we love others, we ultimately do it for ourselves. Pure and true love makes us healthy. It calms our heart rate and improves our mood. We feel good about giving instead of taking. We receive physical, mental, and spiritual benefits when we love absolutely. This is where we will thrive.

LOVE LIMITLESSLY

We are built with the capacity to love without limits. What I mean by this is that there are an infinite number of ways to display love. Leaving an alcoholic spouse may be the best way to love. Allowing your teenager to fail may be the best way to love. Speaking a difficult truth to your friend may be the best way to love. Firing someone may be the best way to love. Saying no may be the best way to love.

But how often do we enable others' destructive behavior, protect our loved ones from natural consequences, avoid the truth because it may hurt someone's feelings, keep someone in a position they're failing at, say yes to something we don't want to do, or spend our time taking care of others instead of ourselves? These are not loving behaviors.

We can love limitlessly when we're doing it from the right place in ourselves. It won't exhaust us, won't be difficult, and won't be fearful. If those are the reactions we're having, we must go back to ourselves and figure out what we're doing wrong.

LOVE SIMPLY

Think of the most difficult relationship you have. What is it about them that bothers you the most? I'll bet you have a whole list full of things they do to annoy you. Get angry with them, and sit in it for a second.

Now think of that person as a baby. Look at their little innocent face and vulnerability. They cannot do anything for themselves. They are totally dependent on you to care for them. They need food and diaper changes. They can't tell you why they're crying but need you to pick them up and hold them tight.

We would be gentle, careful, and patient with the baby. We wouldn't care if they cried or spit up. We'd cuddle them as they screamed. We'd walk them around the house in the middle of the night, singing sweet songs in their ears as we gently bounced them up and down to soothe them.

What if we loved everyone we met like we loved a baby? We could see the innocence in their eyes and give them what they needed. We wouldn't judge their behavior or take it personally. We'd accept their pain and do all we could to soothe them.

Daniel Goleman, author of the book *Emotional Intelligence,* speaks of our ability to not only empathize cognitively with others but also show empathic concern. The distinguishing factor is empathizing with someone like we would empathize with a child. Not only do we feel their distress, but we want to help them.

Everyone is like a child in some area of their life. Everyone needs tender loving care. Everyone needs acceptance.

I've tried this, and it works. Instead of scooping up the nasty repairman in my arms, I see his innocence and understand he doesn't want to be ornery and rude. He's just like a baby who needs love and compassion. I empathize with his busy schedule, dealing with the frustrations of people all day, and hearing their complaints.

And what does it do for me? It creates peace. People respond well to it. Love is born.

But it does even more. It's empowering, peaceful, and freeing.

Instead of taking everyone on as my "project" or letting them know all I know about what they're doing, I back off and simply love. My heart rate drops, I don't create chaos with my words, and my heart is open and free.

It will take courage to give love like this. It will be an intentional act. Don't take their pain in. Don't take their words personally. Just love.

VOCATION

We love both ourselves and others best when we are doing the thing we were created to do. We will enjoy it and be satisfied doing it. It's tough to show a spirit of love when we're in a job we're not good at, don't like, or feel is unimportant.

Being in the flow is a sign of our vocation. This is where we operate best. It's as if we're a machine set up perfectly to do what it was created for. We're cranking out the widgets of our life by stepping into the mold of how we were created and doing *that*. When we're in this state, love flows from us. Our vocation is an extension of our love as we do whatever it is well, enjoy doing it, and serve others.

It's also where we love both ourselves and others best. When we are happy and fulfilled, love comes easily. When we're using our gifts, we share those benefits with others. When we acknowledge our talents, we love and accept ourselves for who we are.

How can your vocation show love?

Summary

Embracing our spiritual health will help us do better for others. This explains why religious organizations across the world have been leaders in providing aid to those in need. When we feel a reason to do something which is beyond ourselves, it's easier to embrace. Sharing our money, resources, and time are ways we do better. Faith motivates, love encourages, hope inspires, gratitude gives, joy spills over, meaning pursues, and purpose fulfills. It becomes easy and natural to think of others.

But doing better is not just about others. When we give, we get more in return. The act of giving blesses us. Thinking about others rather than ourselves takes our minds away from our own troubles. Belief in something or someone greater than ourselves gives great comfort and peace. Love beyond what we can get out of it is what we were created for. It will elevate us to a new level. Better spiritual health will make us feel better.

This leg of the stool, our spiritual health, is just as important as the first two. To be healthy, we must give this as much time and effort as our physical and mental health. Too often, our spiritual health is so weak it's dragging our physical and mental health down. It's not that we're physically unhealthy, it's just that we don't have hope, joy, and meaning in our lives. Because of this, we feel physically tired and mentally drained.

Working on our spiritual health is an individual journey but must be navigated with others. If we go it alone, we'll simply create a church to self. We need others' perspectives to expand our own. We'll become enlightened by the experiences others have had and then weigh them against what's in our own heart. Finding others of a like mind is good. We find agreement and are challenged to expand further.

We are spiritual beings and must pursue our spiritual health. We *need* to understand what we believe and why. Start your journey out of your stuck-ness by finding faith, hope, gratitude, joy, love, meaning, and purpose.

Do better.

Chapter Thirteen

SO NOW WHAT?

It's time to get real with yourself about why you're stuck. Is it your fears, feelings, or beliefs? Are you trying to control things, or is it simply a skill you need to develop? Figuring out why you're stuck is the first crucial step. Once you see the root of being stuck, you're able to do something about it.

What will you do? Only you can decide. Waiting for circumstances to change doesn't work. This is your life, and it's up to you to do something about it. Waiting for others to change doesn't work. If you're not willing to change, why would they? Wishing things would be different doesn't work. Hope is not a strategy.

You must take care of your body, your mind, and your spirit. As you work to strengthen the unhealthy places, you will heal and be free. The answer is there. You just need to find it.

Ask yourself, So now what? No one can answer this question but you. This is good news because you are the best qualified to answer. You will be the only one to take action. And you will live with the results. Your actions will set you free or lead you to another question of, So now what?

This is a lifelong journey for all of us. The beauty of this process is we can grow and become freer each day. We get to decide. The stuck places in our lives are not just bad karma but signposts pointing us toward greater health and freedom.

So now what? What will you acknowledge about why you

are stuck? What steps will you take toward better health? What effort will you go to? How will you get unstuck?

HEALING

When we're stuck and broken, we first need healing. As we heal our body, both our mind and spirit improve too. As we heal our mind, our body and spirit benefit. And as we heal our spirit, our health improves in both our body and mind. Although it may seem we are stuck because of one unhealthy habit, healing ourselves in all three areas will ensure we get completely unstuck.

BODY

With the understanding of our body as a tool, we have to ask every day: What will you do to heal it? What food will heal its ailments? Do you need to cut out carbs, add fruits and vegetables, drink more water, or take supplements? It will take some trial and error, research, and advice from doctors or others who are experts in the body to heal.

What activities does your body need to heal? Do you need to be more active? Less? Do you need to do yoga for stretching, weights to build muscle and bone mass, or a massage to heal from an injury? This too requires information from those who study and work on the body along with patience during the healing process.

Our bodies are resilient and want to heal themselves. Strength and flexibility are not limited to people in their twenties but can be developed all throughout our lives. Chronic pain, genetic predispositions, and unhealthy habits do not have to be permanent conditions.

The key is to be continually asking, So now what? What will you do to heal your body?

MIND

So now what will you do to heal your mind? I used cognitive be-havior therapy, read many books, talked to wise people, and was inspired by others. I had to undo bad mental health habits. It took facing what I was doing and asking why it wasn't working.

We each have control over our minds if we'll take it. It's im-portant to know, however, that our progress will not be linear. Even two steps forward and one step back is still making head-way. Healing our mental state is possible.

What will you do to heal your mind from the stress and strain of broken relationships? Regardless of how dysfunctional those around you appear to be, the strength and quality of your relationships are determined by you. Forgiveness is necessary. Truthful conversations are fundamental. Love is the answer.

What will you do to heal your mind of negative thinking? We were wired for the positive, but so many of us think we're naturally skeptical or see the glass as half empty. Those negative thoughts have been learned. They were created out of fear and are not natural.

What will you do to heal your mind of anxiety? An anx-ious mind is healed by bringing thoughts into order and calm. Not allowing negative "what if" thinking to take hold, breath-ing deeply, and taking responsibility for our emotions heals our mind from anxious thinking. It can become a habit to challenge scary thoughts instead of inviting them to into our minds. The anxious mind can absolutely be healed.

SPIRIT

So now what will you do to heal your spirit? If your spirit has been broken by lost love, hope, or skepticism, it must be repaired. Maybe you need to seek out spiritual teaching. It could be that you need to forgive to heal. A broken spirit can be healed by an empathetic ear. Understanding why the brokenness still exists is a great place to start. Do you need to simply let the sorrow go? Or is it time that will heal the wound? As we embrace this mysterious place and acknowledge how important it is to our overall health, we'll work diligently to get it in order.

Our healing comes when we practice these spiritual practices: faith, gratitude, hope, joy, love, meaning, and purpose.

STRENGTHEN

After we've taken the steps to heal the broken places in our body, mind, and spirit, it's time to be proactive and strengthen them. This strength will be a protector against the next adversity that comes our way. Just as we save money for the future, invest in our friendships, and continually learn new things about the world around us, strengthening our body, mind, and spirit will ensure we stay in the game as things in our life change.

BODY

So now what will you do to strengthen your body? We've been taught a mindset of physical health by the medical community: If something goes wrong, go to your doctor and get it fixed. And, if it ain't broke, don't fix it!

I would like to suggest a new way of thinking.

Since we live in our bodies every minute of every day, and the health of our bodies will significantly impact the value of our life, I suggest we take a proactive approach with them. Instead of waiting until we feel something is wrong, let's adopt the mindset to maintain and improve our bodies every day.

Strength is good. I want the wings of an airplane strong enough to carry the body of the plane into flight, the cables attached to an elevator strong enough to hold the weight of the carriage, and my body strong enough to enjoy my life. For me, that includes lots of activities requiring strength, stamina, and flexibility.

And so I train. I don't do it to look good but to *feel* good. I don't do it to be better than anyone else but to be my best self. If I want to take advantage of opportunities that come my way, I need to be ready for them physically.

How about you? What will you do to strengthen your body? What specific foods will you make sure you eat, and which ones will you avoid to be strong and healthy? How will you ensure you are getting enough rest to be able to handle unexpected stress that comes your way? What exercise routine will you adopt so that you are energetic, strong, and flexible enough to manage your life? What steps will you take to strengthen your body?

MIND

So now what will you do to strengthen your mind? Beyond healing from strained relationships, negative thinking, and anxiety, we can learn mental health skills to successfully navigate life's ups and downs. A strong mind is an intentional mind. It knows how to react properly both for the self and for others. How do you strengthen your mental muscle and move powerfully through the world?

The skills we spoke of earlier are the way to become strong in your mind. Learn to not take things personally, further define your personal boundaries, stop blaming others, get used to delaying gratification, be proactive instead of reactive, ask honest questions of others instead of making up stories, and continue to learn new things your whole life. Each one of these will require practice and persistence to get good at it.

Life will continue to present opportunities to increase our mental abilities. We can look for them in crossword puzzles and card games. We can also embrace them as they show up in disagreements, mental and emotional challenges, and saying no. Instead of cringing at the discomfort, embrace the challenge and strengthen your mental muscle.

SPIRIT

So now what will you do to strengthen your spirit? We strengthen our spirit when we understand our faith is expanded when we discuss it with others. Being part of a faith community goes a long way to strengthen our spirit. As we decide our own positions, we strengthen our faith.

One way to strengthen your spirit is to practice hopefulness when it seems impossible. Regardless of the circumstances, find a way to hope for a better future. A daily gratitude journal is another way to gain spiritual strength. Reminding yourself of the things you're grateful for can become a habit that provides strength in times of difficulty. Choosing joy during the bland times of our lives is another way to build spiritual strength. Make the choice to change your attitude even though it may be difficult.

Looking carefully for the meaning of your life's events is another way to be strong spiritually. The meaning is there, but often we miss it if we're not intentional. Writing it down will solidify the story so you can go back to it and enjoy the meaning again. And pursuing your life's purpose is a way to strengthen your spirit. Instead of playing small and fitting in, owning your gifts and sharing them with others will not only strengthen them but strengthen you too.

And finally, love. Pursuing love in all areas of your life will strengthen your spirit. Love is action. Love is a verb. Love is not simply a feeling but a choice you make. We become strong and resilient as we love others who don't love us back. Our spirit grows and strengthens as we serve those in need and gain a broader perspective. Loving yourself with the purpose of staying strong to give to others is another lifelong pursuit that will strengthen your spirit.

TRIFECTA

There's one more benefit from healing and strengthening our body, mind, and spirit. Although the benefits of taking care of your body, mind, and spirit to heal and strengthen them are enormous, the best part is in how they impact one another.

Healing our body does not just benefit the body. When we're no longer dealing with pain, exhaustion, or inflexibility, our mind will also feel the healing effects. More physical energy will translate into more mental energy to handle emotional struggles. And a rested body is more able to be hopeful, impacting our spiritual health.

As you work to strengthen your body, you deal with discomfort. This builds physical muscle but is also the mindset needed to improve our mental health. You might push a few more miles on your bike and realize being uncomfortable will not harm you. When an unkind word comes your way, you have the ability to push through this discomfort too.

For me, healing and strengthening my body was critical to healing from depression and living a life of purpose. It's been quite a journey. I continue to pay attention to what my body needs on a weekly basis. As I age, enter periods of stress, and pursue goals, different things are required. I may need more sleep some weeks so I can be on my game mentally. I may eat differently from week to week based on my activity level. And I pay attention to new aches and pains, so I don't push too hard.

This trifecta effect also works as we heal and strengthen our minds. Healing from emotional wounds will give us more margin to be hopeful. As we learn to not take things personally, more joy and love will flood into our lives. And as we connect with others, we will have more physical energy. The choices we make in our minds benefit both our bodies and our spirits.

As we mentally own the direction of our life, we will naturally use our physical and spiritual strength to make things happen. The three will feed off each other, enabling us to accomplish our goals. None of these parts work individually as well as in tandem with the others.

And do not miss the benefits of healing and strengthening your spirit. This is a critical component in having a balanced life. Getting in touch with what you have faith in will pour over into the mental health skills necessary to be connected to others. Loving yourself will move you to take care of your body and accept its beauty and imperfections. Choosing joy will be felt both in your body and mind.

To get unstuck, heal and strengthen your body, mind, and spirit. Continue to ask yourself, So now what? Heal yourself by taking care of them. Strengthen yourself by working on them. Then you will be free. Free in your body, free in your mind, and free in your spirit. You will no longer be stuck.

FREEDOM

A FREE BODY

A body healed from its ailments and strengthened is free. It's free to feel good, perform well, and play. It can move without aches and pains. It is free to move through life feeling confident and unencumbered. It is free from exhaustion and filled with energy. It is free from impulse eating and the ensuing guilt. It is free from hormonal difficulties. It is free from brain fog. A free body can take a walk, lift a box, or jump for joy. It gives to others with its energy and talents. It tries new things. It is free to walk around without shame.

A FREE MIND

A free mind is not sidetracked by emotional difficulties. It has mental health skills and continues to learn. A free mind no longer engages in judgment. It is clear. A free mind does not feel angry or frustrated. It experiences failure and learns from it. A free mind does not compare itself to others. It is not anxious or depressed. A free mind does not need to draw attention to itself because it knows its identity. It is connected to others, speaks positively, and has personal boundaries. A free mind takes responsibility, has a strong worth ethic, and is resilient. It is proactive instead of reactive. A free mind laughs easily, rejoices in people's success, and is not jealous. It does not envy others but feels happy with itself. A free mind is connected to the present and not distracted. It does not blame others or dwell on what it cannot control. A free mind lives without fear.

A FREE SPIRIT

A free spirit knows what it believes and stays true to it. It does not get upset when things don't go as planned but allows life to unfold in its own mysterious way. A free spirit lives in community but does not lose itself. It is inspired by others, relies on others, and helps others. A free spirit is grateful for everything. It is hopeful. It experiences each moment as a gift. A free spirit does not argue with reality but finds meaning in it. It holds the possibility of all good things. A free spirit does not follow others but is also deeply connected with them. It believes in the goodness of itself and its connection to all else. A free spirit is respectful, playful, and joyful. It embraces the present without worry or concern. A free spirit connects with the spirit of others and with the spirit of God. Every part of its being displays love.

So Now What?

So Now What? is a lifestyle. It's an attitude. It's constantly asking what your next step should be. It's a belief that there is always another step. There is always an answer.

So Now What? is a journey. It's never done. There will always be something more to do, something more to learn, and something more to experience. It's movement forward instead of being stuck.

So Now What? is a way of life. It starts with love of self. It's a method to heal, strengthen and free your body, mind, and spirit. It will give you freedom.

Freedom to love.

CONCLUSION

So here we are. We understand getting stuck stems from our fears, feelings, beliefs, desire to control, or lack of skills. We've become weak, overwhelmed, and disappointed with our lives. We have the wrong focus, don't know what to do next, and come up with coping mechanisms that are doing nothing to get unstuck. We won't take a step.

But there is a solution. We must believe that the effort will be worth it and that we're capable of the change. We must care for ourselves, stop blaming others, and take action. It will be easier if we get help from others, but the ultimate power is within ourselves.

Free your body, free your mind, and free your spirit. This is all about freedom. When you're finally free, those around you will be too. Love will flow from an unencumbered person who loves fully and fearlessly. You will want to be around yourself, and so will others.

Being stuck isn't a personality flaw, and it certainly doesn't have to be permanent. Every person gets stuck in some way. Part of the joy of life is pushing through difficulty and moving on to new things. Getting unstuck is the way to do it.

Being stuck is our sign that something we're doing isn't working and needs change. When we begin to see the challenges in our lives as gifts, we examine them differently. Just like looking at a new car from the front, the back, and the inside, we walk around the problem, noticing it from all perspectives.

This will take courage.

It seems so much easier to look at other people or situations for the source of our problems. *I'm stuck because he's such a jerk, I'm stuck because I haven't had opportunities everyone else has, I'm stuck because of my gender.* But we're only stuck because of ourselves.

It will take change.

I guarantee the change necessary to get out of the current mud puddle is easier than not changing. This doesn't mean it will be easy; it just means staying where we're at right now is harder in the long run.

It's hard to learn these lessons. It's harder not to.

It's hard to do the work it will take. It's harder not to.

It's hard to change my thoughts and behaviors. It's harder not to.

We must have hope for the process.

But too often, our identity is wrapped up in being stuck. We are the victim. We tell ourselves we're not capable enough, we don't know the right people, or we just can't do the work. We're too sick, sad, and skeptical to move forward. Our ego will tell us things are terrible and then work to prove itself right.

Love is the answer. Love of self and love of others. It begins with loving ourselves enough to care for our body, mind, and spirit. This is not fluffy lingo—it's the nitty-gritty of having a great life. It's the answer to all problems.

Love will heal. It will heal our body, mind, and spirit. It will heal relationships and others. Love has power. Love is necessary.

Love is easy when we are healthy. We can't force ourselves into love. We must become it. We'll transform as our body, mind, and spirit join together, each providing an equal influence on our lives. As we combine these attributes, our potential becomes inexhaustible.

And this is what we were created for.

The never-ending journey of getting stuck and finding our way out is what forms our splendid life. As we become stronger physically, mentally, and spiritually, we pull people along in the wake of our love. We become change agents for others who are sitting in the same puddle we found ourselves in. We can inspire and encourage their growth, as we are inspired and encouraged by others.

It's our choice.

Difficulties and struggles are not only common but necessary. They simply reveal the next step in our journey. We can decide to wallow in them or see them as a signpost for our next lesson. The way out is supposed to be demanding because it's the only way we learn. We can either grab onto our adversity or turn our backs on it.

So now what?
